And Suddenly the Inventor Appeared

TRIZ, the Theory of Inventive Problem Solving

This is an astonishing piece of work. It not only suggests and explains many effective thinking strategies for inventing, it introduces many resources like physics, chemistry, and geometry as tools for solving invention problems and for predicting solutions for problems as yet unrecognized!

In addition, it organizes into a coherent theory, a great many of the ways a thinker can develop skill in approaching a problem where there is "no answer" — where invention is necessary.

And, to put the frosting on the cake, all of this is presented by inviting the reader to learn by doing. The author presents a marvelous variety of real problems where an invention is needed, and asks the reader to use one or another of the **TRIZ** techniques to invent a solution (and reassures "The answer is in Appendix 1"!)

The method is based on a study of thousands of inventions and provides many general principles for reducing a problem to its essentials, reexamining it with fresh eyes, and guiding the would-be inventor to specific areas of technology that are likely to help.

I know of no other approach to inventing that offers such a rich arsenal of both practical and imaginative thinking tools.

In a word, **TRIZ** is a treasure.

Sincerely,

George Prince

George M. Prince
Co-founder of Synectics, Inc.

"A benchmark text, the best introduction to TRIZ (Theory of Inventive Problem Solving) available in English. Lev Shulyak, an inventor who deeply understands and truly loves TRIZ, has created a wonderful translation of Altshuller's work. Because it is written for high school students, I can even understand it!"

Larry R. Smith,
Manager Reliability New Methods,
Reliability and Quality Office,
Powertrain Operations,
Ford Motor Company

"While working with the leading industrial corporations in the world, I became aware of a powerful methodology that has a history of more than four decades, but has only recently been exposed to the western world. This methodology, TRIZ, can help technical innovation in a systematic way and help corporations and individuals reach their peak potential."

Daniel Burrus
Burrus Research Associates, Inc.
Milwaukee, WI 53226

"The true power of TRIZ can not be measured by words alone, for it is such a diverse multidimensional methodology.... The ultimate worldwide impact of TRIZ upon technology driven businesses could easily match the impact of CAD system on new product design."

James P. Dunn
Co-Executive Director, the Center for
Technology Commercialization,
a NASA Regional Technology Transfer Office.

Genrich Altshuller
Developer of TRIZ and,
as Henry Altov, author
of this book

And Suddenly the Inventor Appeared

TRIZ, *the Theory of Inventive Problem Solving*

By Genrich Altshuller (H. Altov)

With original illustrations by Natalie Dronova and Uri Urmanchev

Translated from the Russian by Lev Shulyak

TECHNICAL INNOVATION CENTER, INC.

Worcester, Massachusetts, 1996

Printed in the United States of America

Altshuller, Genrich (Altov, H.)
"And Suddenly the Inventor Appeared"

First Edition, January, 1994
Second Edition, May, 1996

Published by Technical Innovation Center, Inc.
Worcester, MA

Library of Congress Catalog Card: 96-060270
ISBN 0-9640740-2-8

Contents

Part 6: The Amazing World of Tasks
Appendices

Preface to this edition

Two years have passed since the first publication of this translation. Many things have happened with TRIZ theory. It has grown rapidly beyond its original Russian boundaries, reaching the United States, Europe, India, China, Taiwan and more.

Several companies with Russian scientists and TRIZ experts have set their roots in the United States becoming very successful in applying TRIZ technology. A list of American companies providing TRIZ services is located in Appendix 5.

Invention Machine, Inc. (IM) from Cambridge, Massachusetts, was the first Russian company to promote TRIZ in the US in 1991. Today IM offers TRIZ computer software and training. They also provide TRIZ services to companies for solving technical problems.

Ideation International, Inc. (III) based in Southfield, Michigan, was the second US company formed with Russian TRIZ experts. III provides training and consulting, and have developed three Windows-based software solution systems.

Technical Innovation Center, Inc. (TIC), another Massachusetts company, in conjunction with the **Center for Technology Commercialization**, a NASA technology transfer company, became the third major source for TRIZ consultation, training and publications.

Several Russian TRIZ experts – Victor Fey from Detroit, Michigan and Zinovy Roysen from Seattle, Washington – have also formed their own TRIZ consulting groups providing training and problem solving services.

American companies have begun including TRIZ training for engineers. **GOAL / QPC**, based in Methuen, Massachusetts, and Detroit-based **American Supplier Institute** (ASI) are active training organizations promoting TRIZ. In November, 1995, more then 200 people attended an ASI sponsored TRIZ symposium in Detroit. The symposium reaffirmed TRIZ as an important tool for systematic innovation.

Since the initial publication of this book, *Success* and *Machine Design* magazines have published articles on the prosperous application of TRIZ theory in American industries.

Finally, a plan to establish the **Altshuller Institute for Technical Creativity** has been born. The Institute, to be located in Massachusetts, will be a center for the translation and development of TRIZ research and publications. It is hoped the Institute will coordinate certification of TRIZ experts and trainers, and will help develop curriculums to bring TRIZ into

American academic institutions. It will also promote new research on TRIZ to continue its growth in the West, as well as develop new applications in both technical and nontechnical areas.

Thanks to Steven Rodman and Robyn Cutler for their hard work in editing and redesigning this new edition. We are positive that this book will become an even more widespread introduction to TRIZ in the western world.

Lev Shulyak
Worcester, Massachusetts
January, 1996

Preface from the original 1994 edition

"My only intention in this book is to show that the process of solving technical problems is accessible to anyone, important to learn, and very exciting to work through".
H. Altov (Genrich Altshuller)

"Everything should be made as simple as possible, but not simpler."
Albert Einstein

Today technical progress is changing the face of the earth at an ever accelerating pace. Scientists are finding ways to learn more in less time, to remember more and longer, to do things faster, and so on. This creates an enormous need for a constantly growing supply of new ideas and solutions. Moreover, the body of knowledge and the application of this knowledge to solving technical problems is expanding rapidly. How can we manage all this new information and make it useful?

Unfortunately, one of the entrenched beliefs many people hold is that inventiveness is innate and therefore cannot be taught or learned. But we are not consistent. While we resist or ignore teaching technical inventiveness, we do have music and art courses – and schools which take in all sorts of students, not just the extremely talented or artistic.

Thus, we also need schools and courses of study that will teach us to become more inventive or innovative, and will teach us how to solve technical as well as nontechnical problems more creatively. We can do this by providing a new theory for solving technical problems that is based on the experiences of people who have solved real problems. This theory exists and has been used successfully by many people in many countries since it was originated by Henry Altshuller of the USSR in 1946. The system has spread to over 300 schools, teaching many persons of all ages in the former USSR, Finland, Great Britain, Hungary and other countries.

Evidence of its importance can be found in the fact that, in 1978, students of Dnepropetrovsk University and other colleges in the former USSR were required to pass a test on this Theory of Solving Technical Problems.

The system's youngest students are fifth and sixth graders. It is too difficult for youngsters below these grades to learn a theory, since it requires some knowledge of physics to solve the given problems.

The author, Henry Altshuller, is the president of the Inventor's Association of Russia. In 1984 he published the book *And Suddenly the Inventor Appeared* (The Art of Inventing) in which he described the basic parts of his theory in simple language.

If you are an inventor or a person who likes to work out technical problems, then this is the book for you.

You will learn the basic concepts of the Theory of Solving Inventive Problems, (**TRIZ** in the Russian abbreviation). You will find 78 real problems and 27 practical tools to solve them in this book.

This is the first practical book for those in America who want to wet their feet in the ocean of inventing. This is why I decided to translate it.

In some of the answers to the problems, the author refers to inventions that were "patented" in the USSR. These are not real patents as we understand the term. They are so-called "Author's Certificates" – patents only valid in the USSR.

In the translation I tried to preserve the flavor of the original text. Sometimes it was impossible. To adapt this book to American readers, I had to make some changes. Three appendices were added. The first appendix has answers to all the text's problems. The second contains all the methods and tricks the author described in his book in order to solve those problems. The third explains some elements of the author's theory.

My first experience in learning the theory came around 1961. I was designing a very sensitive transducer and was stuck with a problem that did not allow me to make a final formulation of the design. Then the first small book of Henry Altshuller, *How To Become an Inventor*, came out on the market, and this book helped me to solve the "unsolvable" problem in a short time. Since that time I have patented over 20 inventions – many of which were developed because of his theory.

Today, Wayne State University in Detroit is the first American institution to offer courses teaching the Theory of Solving Inventive Problems using Altshuller's concept. Several TRIZ-based computer software products are now available in English.

Those who want to perfect their knowledge in problem solving can do so through courses that are now available at the Technical Innovation Center of Worcester, Massachusetts.

I am positive that you will enjoy reading this book, and I wish you great success.

It is time for our country to regain the leadership in the technical world.

My special thanks to Henry Altshuller, who allowed me to translate his book, to Edith Morgan, Richard Langevin and Alexander Roghach – my copy editors – and to my wife for her patience and her appreciation of the importance of this work.

Lev Shulyak

This edition
is dedicated
to the seventieth birthday
of the author,
Genrich Altshuller

Part 1
The Beginning
of the Theory

Chapter 1
It's Impossible

The first time I saw an inventor was before the Second World War. We lived in Baku, where I was a student in the fourth grade. One day, coming back from school, I saw some repairmen sadly smoking cigarettes next to a broken electric transformer booth. The repairmen were looking at a big black transformer standing on a high brick foundation. The foundation was more than one meter tall, and the transformer looked like an impressive monument. People were waiting for a crane to take the broken transformer down and install a new one.

Later, I did my homework by the light of an oil lamp. We had no electricity that evening, nor the second evening, nor the third. A crane in those days was considered very rare and valuable equipment, and getting one was not a simple matter. The electricians complained about the situation, and did not know when they could finish their job.

I did not realize that an inventor lived in Apartment #11. There were rumors that this neighbor, who was a bookkeeper, on the next day would bring the transformer down from the foundation. Every tenant in our building had a nickname. Some of them were named very respectfully, like "Uncle Kostya," or "Uncle Vlad" — but the bookkeeper was just "Bookkeeper."

On the next day I skipped my last class because I was curious to see how Bookkeeper would lower that heavy transformer. I arrived just in time. At the entrance to our back yard stood a horse carriage full of ice. Workers were

2

unloading the ice and putting it next to the foundation of the transformer.

I must first explain something: In those times we did not have electric refrigerators. Every day, spring to fall, a horse carriage drove from house to house delivering bluish ice blocks. Families purchased the ice and filled wooden boxes with it. Sometimes they filled just pails and pots with the ice.

As the workers carried the ice blocks to the transformer, Bookkeeper stacked them next to the foundation. When the new foundation made of ice reached the same height as the brick one, Bookkeeper placed a wooden board on top of the ice. The workers, using pry bars, slowly, centimeter by centimeter, moved the transformer from the brick foundation onto the ice foundation.

The ice squeaked. However, because the ice blocks were placed very accurately, the frozen foundation did not fall apart. Finally, Bookkeeper personally covered the ice with a piece of cloth. We all stood and watched. Soon a small stream of water appeared on the ground from the melting ice. In the beginning the flow was small. Soon it grew bigger and bigger —because the September sun in Baku is still as strong as in summer.

Everyone in the yard, even a scandalous old man with the nickname "Treasure" (he was sure that he knew where the greatest treasures were hidden, but there was one problem: He did not have money to get there) said that the ice was a very good idea. Uncle Michael — everybody now called the bookkeeper by his first name — sat on his folding chair reading the newspaper. From time to time he would open the side of the cloth to look at the melting ice.

The next morning I ran out into the yard. The transformer was already halfway down. Although it was Sunday, the workers were there. A river of water ran from beneath the cloth cover. I was dumbfounded. Everyone knew that ice melts, and I knew it as well. Nobody had figured out that a transformer could be moved onto a block of ice — and the ice would lower the transformer to the ground. How had Uncle Michael, and no one else, figured it out?

Before, the ice had been just regular ice used only to cool things. But now, ice could replace a crane. Why, ice could probably do other things — and not only ice! Suddenly, the idea struck me that perhaps anything could be used for purposes other than that for which it was created.

A word occurred to me: **Inventing**. I figured that Uncle Michael had created an invention, and therefore he had become an Inventor. Maybe somebody would write an article about him in a newspaper, especially if he could find a way to lift a new transformer onto the brick foundation.

On Monday, however, the crane arrived. The new transformer was put on the foundation, and the old one was taken away. The electricians connected the new transformer, the carpenter rebuilt the booth, and the painters painted it. The job was finished. But I would always remember that under any circumstances, including "hopeless" cases, a solution to a problem could be found.

Something could be invented, and that something could be very simple and surprisingly wonderful.

I received my first patent while in the tenth grade. Later there were other inventions. I worked at the patent office and had meetings with different inventors. I became more and more interested in the mechanics of creativity: How were inventions made? What happens in the head of the inventor? Why does a solution pop-up suddenly?

Do you want to become an inventor? If so, try to solve the following problem:

Problem 1
To break or not to break?

Once, the director of a plant producing electric light bulbs called his engineering staff together for a meeting. He showed them a bundle of letters.

"These are customer complaints," he said. "They are dissatisfied with our light bulbs. We have to increase the quality of our product. I think there is a problem with the pressure inside the bulbs. Sometimes the pressure is higher than normal, sometimes it is lower. Can anybody think how to measure the pressure inside the bulb?"

"It is very simple," one of the engineers said. "Take the bulb, break it and...."

"Break it?!" exclaimed the director.

"To have quality control we will break only one bulb out of a hundred," replied the engineer.

"We have to test *every* bulb," said the director hopelessly. He turned to his engineers and said, "Think it over."

And suddenly the Inventor appeared.

"This problem is for school children," he said. "Open the text book...."

And he explained where to find an almost complete answer to this problem.

What can you suggest? Do you have any ideas on how to measure the pressure inside the light bulb?

After a couple hours of thinking, it is possible to make a list of five to ten solutions for this problem. Usually these ideas are very weak. Often people offer to weigh the lamp. Theoretically, this is possible if you know the weight of the empty lamp and the volume of the glass bulb. You can weigh the bulb with the gas and thus calculate the amount of gas.

In practice this solution is unworkable. There is very little gas in the bulb — one tenth, or even one thousandth, of a gram. It takes a special scale to measure this kind of weight in order to measure deviations from normal. It

4

would take a lot of time to go through these measurements and calculations. It might be good in the lab, but not in the manufacturing plant.

Even an experienced inventor will not find the optimum solution at once. Dissatisfied with a solution, the inventor will continue to analyze idea after idea. The inventor will think about the problem day and night. Everything the inventor sees will be used in a mental attempt to solve the problem.

If it snows, the inventor thinks of cold. *What if we cool the lamp? Gas will become liquid and it will be easy to measure its volume.*

A bus full of people goes by. *Noise, sound.... What if we use ultrasound? The speed of the sound depends on the density of the gas.*

There is a soccer game on TV. *What if a small ball is placed in the bulb? The speed with which it falls depends on the density of gas.*

And so on, day after day, month after month, year after year — sometimes all through life. Sometimes the life of the inventor is not long enough, and other inventors must pickup the problem and continue to search for a solution. "What if we do it this way?" asks the next inventor.

It often happens that, halfway to the solution, the problem is put aside with the conclusion that it cannot be solved, that there is nothing we can do.

You can imagine a scientist saying: "To achieve a speed above the sound barrier we have to study runners and sprinters. How does a good sprinter differ from a bad one? What is the secret of fast running? These are things I need to know."

Runners are all different and, more importantly, the result of such a study cannot be used to build a supersonic machine. Different principles are needed.

This method of trial and error has its roots in ancient times. In essence, it is as old as mankind. Everything changes over time, but the method of trial and error remains the same. One famous scientist of our time, Professor B. Ginsburg, said: "My inventions were the result of sorting out different ideas." At the end of the 20th century the professor looked for answers by sorting out different ideas! This is exactly as it was done two thousand, twenty thousand, two hundred thousand years ago.

So we must look for a better way to solve technical problems.

Technical evolution has its own characteristics and laws. This is why different inventors in different countries, working on the same technical problems independently, come up with the same answer. This means that certain *regularities* exist. If we can find these regularities, then we can use them to solve technical problems — by rules, with formulae, without wasting time on sorting out variants.

Of course, many skeptics scoff. "What you are saying is that we can teach everybody to invent!" I have studied the theory of solving technical problems not one year, not two years, but all my life. In the beginning I worked alone, then others joined me. Through our efforts a new theory has been developed. Books have been published, textbooks written, problems classified, seminars started and schools opened. At the present time, this unique problem solving technique is taught in more than 300 schools in Russia.

The theory of inventing can be taught at any age — but, just as in sports, the earlier the better. We found that professional engineers were the easiest group to teach in the beginning. Because the theory was in its formative stage, experience helped in solving problems. As the theory grew stronger, we began teaching younger engineers, and then students. We later invited high school seniors to participate in college groups. In 1974 a magazine for youngsters started to publish inventors' problems. They were real-life technical problems, very similar to the problem of measuring the pressure inside an electric light bulb. The publishing company received thousands of letters with potential solutions. We analyzed them, made comments on typical mistakes, explained small parts of the theory, and published a new problem in the next issue.

We cannot teach children in kindergarten yet. Our limit has been students in the fifth and sixth grades. To learn the theory of inventing one needs to know a little bit of physics and chemistry, and this is not taught in kindergarten. To overcome this barrier we need to offer fun problems instead of serious ones.

As an example, let's imagine an empty room with only a doll lying on the window sill and two ropes hanging from the ceiling. Our task is to connect the lower ends of the ropes. Taking the end of one rope, a person cannot reach the end of the other rope. Somebody, or something, must help to swing the end of the second rope. This task is set for one person only and there is nobody to help.

The solution could be worked out by children who have no knowledge of physics. The second rope must be moved — but it is too light. It needs some weight at its lower end to develop a pendulum effect. The doll can be the weight. That's all. The problem is solved.

This problem can be made more difficult if we place two balloons with the doll in the room. Balloons are no good as weights because they are too light. Balloons would attract the attention of the child, and the doll would not be considered for a while.

We can even further complicate the task. Let's take all the objects from the room and see if the child can figure out how to use a shoe as a weight. You can see that, on the one hand, this problem is not inventive. Yet, on the other hand, it resembles an inventive problem. We will talk about these similarities later. We can only say now that there are no barriers separating these problems.

In this book we will talk only about technical creativity and inventiveness. This book is not a text book, of course. My only intention is to show that the process of solving technical problems is accessible to anyone, that the process is important to learn, and that it is very exciting.

Chapter 2
Several simple examples

DO IT INVERSELY

DO IT IN ADVANCE

In spite of difficulties, I am going to convince you that some of the following problems are really inventive and the solutions that inventors have found are classified as inventions. You can solve these problems now without learning the theory. You already have enough knowledge and experience to work on them.

Problem 2
There is a "trick" involved

It was a young girl's birthday. One of the guests brought a big box of chocolate candies. The candies were shaped like small bottles filled with thick raspberry syrup. Everybody liked them. One of the guests said, "I wonder how these candies are made?"

"First they made the bottles and then they filled them up with syrup," explained another guest.

"The syrup would have to be very thick, otherwise the candy would not be sturdy enough," said the third guest. "At the same time, the syrup would be very difficult to pour into the bottle. It is possible to warm the syrup making it more liquid. The problem now is that the syrup would melt the chocolate bottle. We would gain in quantity and lose in quality. There would be many defective candies."

7

And suddenly the Inventor appeared.

"I have an idea!" he exclaimed. "I know how to make this type of candy quickly and without defects. The trick is to ...."

He explained everything. Of course the candy could be produced simply. Think it over. What did the inventor suggest?

This problem was published in the youth magazine *Pioneer's Truth*. There were thousands of letters in reply, and almost all of them had the right answer. You probably have already figured out what the trick is: The syrup should be poured into a mold, frozen, and then dipped into the melted chocolate. Icy syrup in warm chocolate is the invention. It was done in the Institute of Chemistry in Estonia.

There is another magazine called *The Official Gazette*. Thousands of inventions are published in this magazine every two weeks. The descriptions of these inventions are sometimes very lengthy, but contain, in the end, the essence of the invention. In any issue of the magazine, three to five percent of the inventions could be developed by school age children. These inventions do not require special knowledge in physics or chemistry. They are small inventions, of course, but they *are* inventions! These ideas are both new and useful.

What would happen if we gave the children even just a little bit of knowledge?!

Problem 3
What place should we choose?

There was an old tower in the central square of a town. One day concern was expressed that the tower was sagging. A committee was established to study whether or not the tower was really sagging. All members of the committee agreed that, in order to take measurements, they needed to find a fixed point — one that would not move and was visible from the tower.

It was possible that the square itself, and the buildings around it, were sagging as well. A park about fifteen hundred feet away had several ledges that were not sagging. However, you could not see the park ledge from the tower because of tall buildings.

"A very complicated situation," said the chairman of the committee, pondering the question. "Maybe we should ask our academicians?"

And suddenly the Inventor appeared.

"Don't bother them!" he said. "Open the sixth grade physics textbook and you will find that...."

And he explained what to look for.

Do you have any ideas?

Probably you have already figured it out. If not, don't be disappointed. Open a physics textbook and find the section on water-leveling devices.

Let's take two glass tubes, set one in the tower and the other in the park on the ledge. Connect them with a flexible hose, and fill the system with water. Because this is a water-leveling device, the level of the water will stay at the same height relative to sea level. Let's mark the levels. If the tower is sagging, the level of water in the tower glass tube will eventually rise above the original mark.

A very smart invention, and only the knowledge of sixth grade physics was used.

Let's work on a problem that is more complex.

Problem 4
"A" and "B" were sitting on a fence

In one of the chemical laboratories, engineers were building a machine to produce a new fertilizer. Two liquid components were to be dispersed separately into a fine mist by this machine. Let's call these liquids "A" and "B." Droplets "A" are supposed to move towards droplets "B," forming new droplets "AB," the new fertilizer according to the chemist's plans. When the machine was turned on, droplets "A" contacted other droplets "A" and droplets "AA" were produced. The same thing happened with droplets "B." But the chemists did not want droplets "AA" and "BB."

"Maybe we should mix liquids "A" and "B" before we make droplets," said one chemist.

"No, we cannot mix them up before dispersion," said another chemist. "I don't know what to do."

And suddenly the Inventor appeared.

"Take the physics textbook. You will find the law that you need in order to solve this problem."

What law do you think he was talking about?

If you look into a physics book you can easily find this simple law. Particles with the same charge repel each other, and particles with a different charge attract each other. Let's charge droplets "A" positive, and droplets "B" negative. When the two streams of droplets come together, we will have only droplets "AB." You can see that ingenuity plus some knowledge of physics will help to solve about five to ten percent of real inventive problems. What if, in addition, we use some special techniques?

Every profession has its own rules, techniques, and tricks that help do the job better, faster and easier. The same is true of solving inventive problems. By the way, we have already learned some of them.

Do you remember **Problem #2** with the candy and syrup? The inventor said, "The trick is...." The "trick" is the *method*, the way to solve the problem. The problem with the candy had two tricks. The first was that everybody wanted to warm the syrup. However, the Inventor offered the **opposite action** — cool, or even freeze, it. The second trick was knowing that frozen syrup melts at room temperature. **The object changed the state of its physical property**. The same transformation happened in the problem that the Bookkeeper solved. The ice melted and the transformer was slowly lowered.

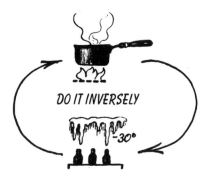

Many methods are based on the application of physical effects and laws. Methods differ from physical effects and laws because methods aim at solving technical-inventive problems. Physical law states that matter can be transformed from one state into another. The method specifies that, during such transformations, the physical properties of the matter change dramatically, and these transformations can be used to solve many specific technical problems.

These are two very powerful methods:

Method #1: Do it inversely, and Method #2: change the state of the physical property.

In any given issue of *The Official Gazette* we can find inventions made using these methods. For example, Patent #183122: "Method for unloading raw granulated sugar from tankers." To speed up the process, the sugar is first mixed with water to make it liquid, and then pumped into a storage silo. The liquid sugar is then dried back to granulated sugar.

Another example, Patent #489938, is a method for restoring the free-flowing characteristic of bulk material in storage. The inventor suggested further freezing it with liquid nitrogen instead of the usual method of heating it with steam. The nitrogen breaks the ice between particles and then evaporates as a gas.

The inventor used two methods. First, **Do it inversely** — freeze the material instead of heating it. Second, **Change the state of the physical property** of nitrogen. The nitrogen is at first liquid and then becomes a gas.

Now try a problem that you can solve yourself.

Problem 5
It can disappear by itself

In the past, people used unspillable inkwells. If we fill such an inkwell with sand, how can we remove the sand from the inkwell later? Foundry engineers once faced a similar problem. Forged metal parts needed to be cleaned. Sandblasting machines were used for this purpose. Sand cleans parts — and lodges in cavities. Now we have to remove the sand from the parts. When the parts are big and heavy, it is inconvenient to turn them over and shake the sand out.

"Maybe we can somehow cover all the holes?" suggested one engineer. "No, it's too much extra work. I cannot see the solution. The sand does not come out of the cavities by itself."

And suddenly the Inventor appeared.

"Yes," he said, "the sand can disappear by itself. What we have to do is make sand particles out of...."

What should the sand particles be made of?

Notice that all the previous problems belong to different technological fields, but inventors used the same techniques to solve them: **Method #1: Do it inversely,** and **Method #2: Change the state of the physical property.**

Here is one more problem:

Problem 6
There is a patent

There is a need to make many holes 10mm in diameter in a rubber hose. It is not hard to punch or drill the holes except that the hose is very flexible. It stretches, compresses and bends. So, making the holes accurately is a complicated task. The supervisor tried to burn the holes with a heated iron rod, but the edges of these holes were uneven and brittle.

"Nothing can be done! How annoying!" exclaimed the supervisor, almost crying.

And suddenly the Inventor appeared.

"Do not cry!" he said. "It is very simple! There is an English Patent #1268562 where the inventor offered...."

What was in this patent? Think about it.

You have familiarized yourself with only a couple of methods. There are about a hundred of them, some surprising and ingenious. You will agree with me after you solve another problem.

Problem 7
What kind of detectives are they?

A company purchased sunflower oil. The delivery was arranged by tank-cars. Every tank-car had a capacity of 3000 liters (750 gallons). The buyer suddenly discovered that every time the tank was unloaded there was a shortage of almost 30 liters. The buyer checked the measuring devices and all were in order. He checked out the seals on the upper hatch, and the leakage of the tank. Nothing was wrong. He even considered the thin film of oil on the inside walls of the tank, as well as changes in the oil's temperature. There was nothing that

11

could account for the difference.

Some experienced detectives were asked to investigate the problem and they found nothing. The truck never stopped during delivery, and the driver never poured oil out of the tank. Even the detectives were puzzled.

And suddenly the Inventor appeared.

"What kind of detectives are you?" he asked. "It's all very simple. We have to think for awhile." Then he explained what was happening.

What do you think was happening?

This problem was published in a youth magazine. The publisher got thousands of letters from students in schools and colleges, and even from engineers. The authors of two letters were policemen. There were mountains of letters, but none had the right answer.

The detectives could easily have discovered the secret had they known one of the inventor's tricks: **If it cannot be done now, it should be done in advance**.

It turned out that the driver hung a bucket inside the tank when it was empty. The vendor filled the tanker with oil. At the same time, the bucket was filled. The truck went to the buyer's site and was unloaded. The bucket full of oil was still hanging inside the tank, and the driver of the truck removed it later.

This is Method #3: Do it in advance. It is often used by inventors.

Let's look at a problem in medicine. A plaster cast is very difficult to take off without touching the skin. An inventor offered to insert a rubber tube containing a thin saw blade underneath the cast. When the time comes to remove the cast, the doctor takes a handsaw frame, connects it to the ends of the blade, and cuts the cast from the inside out.

DO IT IN ADVANCE

Chapter 3
Technical Contradictions

We have learned three methods, or procedures, so far. You may think that this is going to be simple — just learn hundreds of methods and you can solve any problem. Unfortunately, it is much more complicated. Consider the following example:

There are machines that make welded steel pipes of a large diameter. In the shop, workers hang up big rolls of steel ribbon. The end of this ribbon is inserted into the machine which turns the ribbon into pipes. Welded pipe comes out of the machine at a speed of two feet-per-second. Everything is fine, except that the pipe must be cut to a specific length.

Let's say that we need to make pipes that are 12 feet long. This means every six seconds a pipe must be cut. A rotating cutting disk blade starts to cut the pipe as soon as the pipe reaches 12 feet. The blade travels along with the pipe as it comes out of the machine. After it cuts the pipe, the blade returns to its starting point. This entire process needs to be accomplished in less than six seconds.

In order to cut the pipe faster, a very powerful cutting mechanism is needed. Because such a mechanism must be large and heavy, it will lose speed traveling along the pipe. If we make the cutting mechanism lighter and smaller, in order to gain speed, it cannot cut the pipe as fast as needed. This forms a vicious circle.

To solve this kind of problem, engineers usually use a compromise solution. As a result of such a compromise, the cutting mechanism neither cuts fast nor moves fast, so the pipe comes out of the machine 1.5 times slower than it should — a very disappointing situation.

You have probably already found the solution: **Do it in advance** — cut the steel ribbon before it reaches the machine. However, this will not solve the problem because now we will lose time feeding the machine for each pipe. The high output of this pipe-welding machine depends upon a continuous, unbroken process.

This problem remained unsolved for a long time. By using various tricks, engineers increased the speed of the cutting blade but lost the accuracy of the pipe lengths. Some pipes came out longer, others shorter. A complicated electronics system was designed and the accuracy rose — along with production costs and maintenance.

The Inventor appeared, of course, and offered to use two methods: **Method #3: Do it in advance** *and* **Method #4: Do a little less.**

The meaning of the fourth method is: **If an action cannot be done completely, it must be done partially.** This means that the ribbon should be notched, not cut. After the pipe is welded to its required length, a slight jerk will be enough to separate it from the next pipe. It is a wonderful solution, isn't it? The "flying" disk blade is eliminated completely. The pipe goes through an electric magnet. An impulse of current, a sharp break, and the pipe is separated.

As you can see, the "trick" is to have a combination of two methods. Separately, the two methods will not produce the necessary result.

Ten thousand two-method combinations can be produced out of one hundred individual methods! You can imagine the number of solutions we can get if we use a combination of three, four, or five methods. So, let us stop solving problems by sorting out different solutions or using the trial-and-error method.

Some methods of solution were known even at the end of the 19th century. Various specialists have since made itemized lists of 20 to 30 methods. If we go one step further — not only adding new methods, but classifying and combining them — we can solve many more problems.

It was found that single methods can only be utilized in limited areas. Therefore, it is still difficult to get rid of the trial-and-error method.

What if we try to look at technical problems from a different angle in order to understand how the problems came about? What is the definition of an "inventive problem" or a "technical problem?"

Let us look again at the problem of the pipe-making machine. It is a complicated machine with many mechanical systems and parts. As efficiency in one system is increased — the machine welding the metal pipes — the whole became more productive. However, immediately a technical contradiction appeared: The machine welds the pipe much faster than the cutting mechanism can cut the pipe.

To solve this new problem — the faster the welding process, the more difficult the cutting process — an attempt was made to increase the capacity of the cutting mechanism. Again, a technical contradiction appeared: In order to gain speed in cutting the pipe, a more complex and heavy cutting mechanism is needed. Of course, this heavier and more complex cutting mechanism is slower to move down the pipe, again slowing the process as a whole.

Technical systems are similar to living organisms. They consist of *interrelated parts*. **Changing one part of the system may have a negative effect on the system's other parts.**

An improvement in one part of a system that impairs other parts of the system, or adjacent systems, creates a *Technical Contradiction* — and making an invention requires removing Technical Contradictions.

An inventive solution always has two requirements:
**(1) *Improve* a single part or characteristic
of the system without
(2) *impairing* other parts or characteristics of the system
or adjacent systems.**

Problem 8
Vehicle for the planet Mars

In a science fiction story about space exploration an expedition to Mars was described. The space ship landed in a rocky valley and the astronauts promptly prepared their vehicle for a trip on the planet surface. This special vehicle was designed with big inflated tires. On the very first steep slope the vehicle tipped over.

And suddenly.... No, unfortunately, the Inventor could not appear in this story. What do you think the Inventor would have offered?

Keep in mind that the astronauts had no way of changing the tires.

This problem was also published in a youth magazine. In the majority of the letters received, the answer was to suspend a heavy weight underneath the vehicle. The center of gravity of the vehicle would become lower and increase the vehicle's stability.

Do not rush to express your idea yet. Let's first make an analysis of the other suggestions. Now we have a criterion for our evaluation. Was the technical contradiction removed or not?

The weight suspended underneath the vehicle will increase stability, but at the same time will impair its mobility to travel. The clearance will be less and cause the weight to strike rocks and the ground more often. A technical contradiction!

15

Here are some of the other ideas and suggestions:

  a. Partially deflate the tires, so they will be half-full.
  b. Install an extra tire on each side of the vehicle.
  c. Have some members of the crew lean out of the vehicle, to maintain balance....

It is not so difficult to see that in each of these ideas we gain something while we lose something else. Deflating the tires reduces the speed of the vehicle. Additional tires make the vehicle more complicated — and we have no means of doing that on Mars. Asking the astronauts to do acrobatic tricks is not a justifiable risk. Because of the difficulty of avoiding contradictions, one of the readers wrote: "Nothing I can think of can be done. Let the astronauts walk."

Can you imagine a sailor who does not know that it is necessary to avoid reefs and cliffs? The inventor is like that sailor when he does not know that he must remove a technical contradiction.

Do you remember the problem about measuring the pressure inside the electric light bulb? The idea to break the bulb was patented, although in reality an invention was not created because the contradiction was not removed. The more bulbs we break, the more accurate the test will be, and the more broken bulbs we will get.

Before you say, "I have solved an inventive problem!"
ask yourself, **"What kind of contradiction have I removed?"**

It is not difficult to suspend a weight underneath a vehicle. The idea is to suspend it as low as possible. Now we have another problem. A low suspended weight will reduce clearance between the vehicle and the ground. The desire to solve this problem without using "inventive tricks" will not improve the mobility of the vehicle.

Let us try a new method, a new trick: We will place the weight very low, in fact, right next to the ground — not outside the vehicle, but inside. We will hide the weight inside — the tires! We will insert steel balls or round stones, and they will roll over....

This is Method #5, called "Matreshka." Matreshka is a doll that has a smaller doll inside it, and another doll inside of the second doll, and so on. To save space it is possible to place one object inside another.

A patent to this effect was issued in Japan to improve the stability of fork trucks and autocranes.

The problem and the answer are like two banks of a river. An attempt to guess the answer is like jumping from one bank of the river to the other. Technical contradictions, and methods to remove them, work as a bridge. The theory of solving technical problems is similar to the science of building invisible bridges that carry thoughts leading to new ideas.

By the way, contradictions and methods should be compared to support columns of the bridge. It is not easy to jump from one column onto another. In addition to columns, we need top panels so that we can walk from one side to the other. We need a special approach to get from task to contradiction, and from contradiction to the method (trick). Then we can walk step-by-step from the problem statement to the answer.

We will talk more about the parts of the bridge later. What is very important to understand is:

The inventor must find and remove technical contradictions.

The theory of solving technical problems begins with this very simple statement.

Chapter 4
Think For Yourself

So far you have learned five methods of solving different problems:

1. **Do it inversely**
2. **Change the state of the physical property**
3. **Do it in advance**
4. **Do a little less**
5. **"Matreshka"**

You have also learned that physical effects and phenomena can be used in the methods described above. And, finally, you have a very reliable indicator by which to evaluate your idea. A good inventive idea will certainly remove contradictions.

I will give you several problems as an exercise. Remember, do not sort out ideas. Use the methods you have learned; i.e., physical effects and knowledge about contradictions.

Problem 9
One as good as many

Once upon a time, in a laboratory, a device was built to study the movement of droplets of liquid fertilizer to be sprayed from an aircraft. Air rushed

18

through a pipe carrying millions of droplets. However, this device produced only very small droplets.

During the experiment it was found that droplets of larger sizes should be tested as well.

"Let's purchase several devices," offered one of the engineers.

"It will take more time than we have. Besides, it is too expensive," contradicted another engineer. "Twenty tests will require twenty different sprayers."

And, of course, the Inventor suddenly appeared.

"One sprayer will work as well as many different sprayers," he said. "The dimensions of the droplets could be changed if...."

He explained what should be done.

What do you think?

Probably problem #9 looks simple to you. Although the next few problems are more complicated, I think you will work them out.

Problem 10
To make water softer

Once, a famous coach — a former champion diver — complained to his colleague: "It is difficult to work today. Dives are becoming more and more complicated. We have to think of new combinations, and try them. The problem is that the large number of unsuccessful landings has increased diver injuries. The water is not so soft when you fall from a tall tower. Sometimes I feel that a diver could make new dives, but often is afraid to get injured and not able to enter the competition."

"There is nothing we can do," his colleague said. "This is the nature of the sport we are committed to. There are injuries in my team as well during unsuccessful dives."

And suddenly the Inventor appeared.

"There will be no more injuries. We will make the water softer. What we have to do is...."

What do you think we have to do with the water to make it softer and eliminate injuries during dives?

Problem 11
Everlasting paint

The president of a furniture company said to his engineer: "During the last year we sold one hundred sets of furniture to kindergartens. Unfortunately, the customers are complaining that the kids have stripped or scratched the paint off the furniture."

"This is not our problem," said an offended engineer. "You can scratch the hardest of paints. This has nothing to do with us. Maybe they should buy unfinished furniture."

"No," said the president. "It is good to have colorful furniture in kindergartens. Perhaps we can find a paint that will penetrate deep inside the wood?"

"This is a fantasy!" laughed the engineer. "Thousands of times people have tried to impregnate wood with paint with very poor results. You know that."

And suddenly the Inventor appeared.

"No, this is not a fantasy!" he exclaimed. "It takes some ingenuity and bravery to solve this problem. The trick is...."

What do you think the trick is?

Chapter 5
Superimpose That Which is Not
Superimposable (Join what is not joinable)

The hunted fox, if you will believe Baron Munchausen, found a way to jump out of its own skin. Let's leave this hunting story to the Baron's conscience. At the same time, a similar story happened with an inventing problem. We started to hunt for the answer, we found technical contradictions, and just when it seemed that the answer was at hand — suddenly the answer disappeared!

Even if you hold the technical contradiction with strong hands, there is no guarantee that you will find the answer. The same technical contradiction could be removed by using different methods.

Technical contradictions are derived from **physical contradictions**. In other words, at the heart of every *technical* contradiction is hidden a *physical* contradiction. It looks like this: One part of a technical system should have the characteristic "A" to perform a certain action, and it should also have the contradictory characteristic "anti-A" to perform the opposite action.

> A *Technical Contradiction* usually relates to the whole system,
> or to several parts of the system. A *Physical*
> *Contradiction* relates only to one part of the system.

Understanding this statement will significantly increase your chances of getting to the correct answer.

Let's look at **Problem #5** — removing sand from the forged parts. The physical

21

contradiction in this problem is: "Particles should be hard in order to clean parts, and at the same time not hard (liquid or gaseous), in order to be removed from the area inside of the parts." As soon as this kind of contradiction is formulated, the answer becomes obvious. We have to apply **Method #2: Changing the state of physical properties** — and nothing else! Let's make particles out of dry ice. Hard particles will clean the parts, and later turn into gas and evaporate.

In **Problem #6**, how to make holes in the rubber hose, the physical contradictions are almost the same. The pipe should be hard in order to drill holes in it, and should be soft to preserve elasticity. The method is the same. We have to freeze the pipe, or fill it with water and freeze the water. After the holes are made, the pipe or water should be heated.

There are certain rules that allow us, during the analysis of the problem, to go from a technical contradiction to a physical one. In many cases the physical contradiction could be formulated from the description of the problem itself.

Problem 12
Droplets on the screen

The welding process was studied in a research laboratory. Scientists were interested to find out how a metal rod would melt in an electric arc, and how this arc changes during this process. They turned the power on, set the arc and filmed what happened. When they reviewed the movie they found that only the arc was visible. The arc is brighter than the droplets of metal, and therefore the droplets could not be seen. It was decided to repeat the experiment. In the new experiment a second arc was ignited to light up the droplets. A movie was taken again. Now only the droplets were seen on the screen. The original arc was not visible on the screen at all. The scientists pondered, "What should we do?"

And suddenly the Inventor appeared.

"A typical physical contradiction," he said. "The problem is...."

What kind of physical contradiction is it, and how can we remove it?

If you have read carefully the conditions of the problem, you can easily formulate the physical contradiction. The second arc should be there in order to see the metal droplets, and it should not be there in order to see the first arc.

Technical contradictions are usually formulated in very mild terms. For example, in order to increase the speed of a truck we need to reduce the cargo weight. The speed is in *conflict* with the weight. However, it is possible to arrive at a compromise solution. In physical contradictions, the conflict is very strong. Fortunately, the world of inventing has its own rules: **The higher the degree of the conflict, the easier it is to determine and remove it.**

The arc that lighted up the droplets *should* be and *shouldn't* be. This means that it should be there for some period of time, and it should not be there for another period of time. On and off, on and off. On some frames we will see droplets, on others — only the arc. During the film demonstration both objects will come out on the screen, and we will see the arc and the droplets.

This is Method #6: Conflicting requirements are separated in time or in space.

Do you remember the problem about the welded pipes? The steel ribbon was cut partially in some areas and was not cut in other areas. There is a trickier way to superimpose that which is not superimposable: **Give one characteristic to the whole object, and the opposite characteristic to its parts.** At first, it seems that this is impossible. Indeed, how can you build a white tower out of black bricks?

Take, for example, the chain drive for a bicycle. Each of its elements is rigid, but the whole chain is flexible. In short, physical contradictions that require us to superimpose that which is not superimposable do not lead to a dead end. On the contrary, they facilitate and make easier the process of searching for the best solution.

For another example, consider *Problem #10* — **How to make water softer**. This is a difficult problem. It is not clear yet how to start. Let's first try to formulate the physical contradiction. The pool should be filled with water, and at the same time the pool should be filled with something that is softer so the diver will not be injured during the jump. What is softer than water? Gas or air. The conclusion is: The pool should be filled with....

It seems that we have come to a dead end. The water supports the diver, but it is "tough, hard" during the dive. The gas is "soft," but you cannot jump into a pool filled only with gas or air (the pool is actually "empty"). Now, when we reveal the contradiction, we can see a spark of the answer. Let's have both water and gas in the pool. Let the diver jump into a mixture of water and gas — gaseous water. This is exactly how Soviet inventors got their Patent #1127604. In this patent water is saturated with air bubbles before the jump. The contradiction is removed. Gaseous water is still water, even though you don't feel it in the same way.

Notice the zig-zag path made on our way to the solution. The pre-existing condition for the problem is only the existence of water — and therefore the answer is not clear. We took one step back from water to anti-water (gas, air). It seemed the problem became more complicated. The next step is very important: Combine water and anti-water (water and air, hard and soft, rigid and flexible, hot and cold).

As we said before, it *can* be done — in a time or a space frame.

Problem 13
Thick and thin

A factory received an order to manufacture a large quantity of glass sheets of oval shape one millimeter thick. First, rectangular plates were cut, and then the corners were ground to the required oval shape. Because the glass was very thin, there were many broken sheets.

"We should make the sheets thicker," said the worker to his supervisor.

"We can't," said the supervisor. "We have orders only for sheets one mm thick."

And suddenly the Inventor appeared.

"Physical contradiction!" he exclaimed. "Our sheet glass should be both thick and thin. This contradiction can be separated in a time frame. The glass stock will be thick during the machining period."

What do you think about it?

Problem 14
How to get out of a dead end

A company started the production of a new machine. Very soon the shop faced an unexpected problem. One component of this machine was to be made out of a special steel plate. The plate stock should be electrically heated to 1200^0 C. Then the heated plate would be placed under a press to shape it into its required form. During this process it was found that when the steel plate was heated over 800^0 C it became damaged due to the harmful effect of air.

The supervisor called for a meeting immediately.

"The situation is just like in a fairy tale. Going to the right is getting into trouble; going to the left is getting into even more trouble. The plate stock should be heated to 1200^0 C, otherwise it cannot be formed, and at the same time it cannot be heated over 800^0 C in order not to damage the surface," he said.

"It is very simple!" said one of the youngest engineers. "We will heat it to 1000^0 C, the intermediate temperature."

"That's no good," objected the old master. "The plates will be damaged because they still will be heated beyond their acceptable temperature, and forming cannot be done because the temperature is not high enough."

"It is an intricate task," said the supervisor. "We've got to solve this problem now."

And the Inventor appeared here.

"I have the solution," he said.

What do you think the Inventor offered?

Problem 15
Stubborn spring

Imagine that you have to compress a spiral spring 4" long and 2" in diameter, place it inside a book, and close the book in such a way that the spring will not unwind and yet still be ready to expand at any time. A similar situation happened when engineers were assembling a device. It was necessary to compress a spring, place it inside the device, and close the cover. How can this be done?

"We will tie it with a string," said one of engineers. "Otherwise you cannot do anything with this stubborn spring."

"This is no good," objected the other engineer. "The spring inside the device should be free."

And suddenly the Inventor appeared.

"Everything is fine!" he said. "The spring should be free and it should not be free, compressed and not compressed. Once we have a contradiction, we have an inventive task."

How would you solve this problem?

Part 2
The Era of Technical Systems

Chapter 6
Boat + Boat

In many books about the history of technical evolution, the 19th century is called "The Century of Steam." Historians in the first half of this century called this "The Century of Electricity." What name is appropriate in light of developments in the second part of our century? So far we do not have just one opinion. It could be: "The Century of the Atom," or "The Century of Space Exploration." Maybe, "The Century of Chemistry?" Or... "Electronics?"

If an engineer living at the beginning of the 20th century could see our life today, that engineer probably would be surprised at the number of familiar machines. These machines would differ primarily in scale compared with their ancestors. Cars the size of horse carriages have become big tractor trailer trucks. An airplane that could only carry two or three people has become an airbus carrying 300 to 400 people. Ships have become floating cities. Turbines, cranes, buildings, research laboratories — everything has become ten times bigger.

Dozens of old trucks in the past are now equal to one super-truck carrying their combined loads. Yes, the gross weight is the same, but servicing and maintaining one supertruck takes fewer people. Loading and unloading trucks take much less time as well. Many of today's inventive problems have appeared because of this development.

Let's look at a related problem:

26

Problem 16
After an emergency landing

A huge transport airplane made an emergency landing on a field 200 miles from the airport. The airplane was unloaded and inspected. Cracks, dents and damage to the outside were found. It was necessary to move the airplane to the shop for repairs. Because the airplane weighed more than one hundred tons, it had to be brought to the shop carefully to prevent additional damage. The experts got together. It would not be such a big problem if only the airplane was smaller.

"You should not think so much!" said a student-apprentice.

Nobody had asked him to the meeting, but he had come anyway. He had an idea, and he wanted to present it. "There is nothing we can do without a dirigible. We have to hook the airplane to the dirigible and ...."

"Young fellow," one of the experts sadly said. "We do not have a dirigible of that capacity. Besides, we cannot lift the airplane into the air. So, forget the dirigible."

And suddenly the Inventor appears.

"You're wrong," he said. "We *do* need a dirigible, and we *do not* need a dirigible. We have to lift the airplane — and we don't have to lift it."

He then explained how we could resolve these contradictory requirements.

Can you guess what the Inventor offered?

The sizes of machines have increased rapidly. They have increased by factors of two, ten, and even a hundred times.

Growth, however, is not unlimited. The time comes when further growth is both uneconomical and non-beneficial. At that point, if two machines are joined together, a new *system* appears. This new system then begins to grow and evolve like the individual machines before it.

Let's recall the history and the development of the ship. The first boat was powered by two paddles. The first ship had one row of oars. Then larger ships had two, three and four rows of oars.

In ancient Rome, a ship was built with thirty rows of oars! It was very difficult for oarsmen to coordinate their rowing. Besides, the paddles were long and heavy. The distance between the uppermost rows and the water was more than 60 feet.

Later people started to build ships comprised of paddles and a sail. As time passed, the size of the ships increased, and the number and size of sails increased instead of the number of paddles. Gradually, paddle-sail vessels were turned into sail-paddle vessels, and later into sailing ships. Then, sailing equipment started to evolve. First there was one mast, and then two masts, and so on. The size of sails increased, as did the number of sails on each mast.

Then came the next step: The steam engine was developed and the first sail-steamship was built. Soon, the process repeated again. Sail-steamships were turned into steam-sail vessels, and later into steamships.

Every time system A combines with system B, a new system AB emerges. This new system AB has, in principle, new characteristics — new qualities that neither A nor B had before. Even when a new system is formed out of the simple A + A, the result is not equal to 2A, but to something bigger. For example: One boat plus one boat combined into a system is not equal to two boats. It is a catamaran. The system *catamaran* is more stable than just two separate boats.

This very important feature of systems can be easily traced in the next problem about weevils.

Problem 17
A thermometer for weevils

Once upon a time, scientists got together to discuss a problem about weevils. It was found that the conditions of existence for this small beetle had been studied very little. Nobody knew, for example, what the body temperature of a weevil was.

"The weevil is very small," said one scientist. "You cannot use a regular thermometer."

"We have to design a special device," agreed another scientist. "This will require a lot of time."

And suddenly the Inventor appeared.

"It is not necessary to develop a new device," he said. "Take an ordinary...."

What do you think the Inventor offered?

This problem was published in *Pioneer Truth* magazine, and only one word was added in the description of the problem, *glass.* The Inventor said: "Take an ordinary glass...."

Half of the answers offered by readers were: "Take a glass, fill it up with water, throw the weevil into it, and measure the temperature with a regular thermometer." This is not the correct answer. One small weevil cannot change the temperature of the water. The confusion was in the word "glass." Once we have a *glass*, it should be filled with *water* because this is its prime purpose.

In trying to solve inventive problems, "word-traps" can be found often. Such words lead you to wrong ideas. Therefore, in the Theory of Solving Inventive Problems, there is one very important rule: **All special terms must be replaced with simple**

words. This is Method #7.

For instance, if a "micro-adjustable screw" is mentioned in the problem, it should be replaced with words like "adjustable rod that has a very precise movement." The word "screw" disappears, and immediately it becomes clear that the solution may not be connected with the screw motion of the device.

Meanwhile, let's return to our problem. It is necessary to take a glass (or small box, or plastic bag), fill it up with weevils, and measure the temperature with a conventional thermometer. A hundred weevils will create a system that has new characteristics. The size of that system is much greater than the size of its separate parts. Therefore it will not be difficult to measure the temperature of the weevils.

In every issue of *The Official Gazette* we can find technical innovations that were done by incorporating similar or different objects into one system.

This is Method #8: **Incorporating similar or different objects into one system.**

For example, let's consider Patent #408586. Years ago boilers were lined up separately. Now they are placed into one block. The construction became simpler, the pipe length was reduced, and the block needed only one chimney.

Another example: Animal feed in a silo gives off a lot of heat, therefore it is necessary to cool the silo. Barns for domestic animals need to be heated. In Patent #251801 the author offered to combine the two enclosures. Heat from the silo now heats the barns.

Another example: If we take a motorboat and install a snowmobile (or motorcycle) on it, there is no new invention. However, an American inventor got Patent #3935832 for a vehicle that is a boat and a snowmobile at the same time. It uses only one engine, the one from the snowmobile. This is a *new* system.

A hunter, on some occasions, would like to have two rifles with different charges — bullets and pellets. To go hunting with two rifles is not convenient. The hunter needs to use one rifle, and then suddenly needs to use the other. Often, the hunter doesn't have enough time to switch them. What if the two rifles were tied together? In the past, that is exactly what people did. Later they figured out that two rifles tied together share many common parts — and these parts could be eliminated. Indeed, why does this double rifle need two rifle butts? After the extra parts were eliminated, the result was the double-barreled gun.

One more ingenious example: Waste materials — ash and clinker — are created at metallurgical plants and are eliminated through pipes by water. A hard crust develops on the inside walls of these pipes. This crust must usually be removed by hand. Engineers tried to solve this problem for a long time. Other engineers tried to solve the different problem of protecting the inner surface of coal-waste pipes from excess wear. Sharp particles of coal scratch the metal, making the pipes difficult to protect. Inventor M. Sharapov offered to form a common single system out of these pipelines. First, the line would pump ash and clinker slurry that would develop a crust inside the pipes, then it would switch to the coal waste slurry that would clean the pipes. The cycle then repeats. The problem is solved.

To form a new system, one should unite objects in such a way that a new feature appears.

Now we will offer another problem as an exercise.

Problem 18
The other way around

A plant got an order to manufacture glass filters of one meter in diameter and two meters high. Holes were to be made evenly throughout the filter. Engineers looked at the drawings and were shocked. Thousands of tiny holes had to be made in every filter.

"How should we make these holes?" the chief engineer asked his subordinates. "Are we going to drill them?"

"Maybe we should make them with long red-hot needles?" a young engineer said uncertainly.

And suddenly the Inventor appeared.

"We need neither drill bits nor needles. Everything should be done the other way around," he said. "Take...."

What do you think the Inventor offered?

Here is a hint: Do it the other way around. We will not make holes in the cylinder, but make the cylinder out of... holes. Take glass tubes, bundle them, and there is a cylinder with holes. Or, take glass rods, bundle them, and there is a filter with holes between the rods. This filter is very simple to assemble and disassemble.

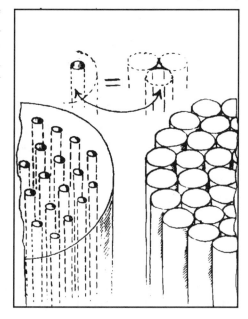

By the way, notice that in this example two methods were used. The solid cylinder was replaced with many small tubes or rods, bundled together.

This is Method #9: Fragmentation and/or consolidation.

Fragmentation and consolidation (also, process and anti-process) are used often in solving inventive problems. When there is a two-part contradiction — something *should* be, and *should not* be — there is a two-part "key" to solve it.

Chapter 7
Something About the Systems

If the amoeba could speak, it would say: "My single-cell ancestors lived on the Earth billions of years ago. Now, everything consists of single-cell combinations. Wood, for example, is a combination of cells. A human being is also a combination of cells. This means that the Era of Cells is continuing!"

With all due respect to the single-cell speaker, we should object. Wood and human beings have different characteristics than single cells. The wood, as well as the human being, are *systems* of cells. There is no longer an actual Era of Cells, there is an Era of Systems.

Growth of systems by development and complication is a universal law. In the technical world, development goes from a *cell* to a *system*. An automobile is a *cell*, the automobile industry is a *system*. A telephone is a *cell*, the telephone industry is a *system*.

When a single cell becomes part of a system, it performs more efficiently, and develops faster. At the same time, the cell depends on the system and cannot exist without it.

Contemporary technology is a technology of systems. Its "cells" are different devices, machines and equipment. They function inside the system. Therefore, some people in the second part of the 20th century call this "The Century of Technical Systems."

There is a strict subordination inside a technical system. An electric bulb in a car is subordinated to the electrical system of the car. The car is subordinated to the car industry, which includes millions of cars, roads, gas stations and repair stations.

Every technical system has a "superior" system above (*super*system) and a "subordinate" system below (*sub*system). Any change in a hierarchical system effects both systems. A technical contradiction emerges because somebody forgets this law. One part of the system gets an advantage over its "superior" or "subordinate" system. Therefore, it is necessary to consider the interests of not only the system that needs to be improved, but also the interests of the subsystems and the supersystem.

Let's look at a specific problem to learn how to consider these interests.

Problem 19
Let's do it without telepathy

Once, a new car stalled on a highway. The confused driver was trying to explain to the passenger: "It is bad luck. I ran out of gas. I forgot to look at my gas gauge."

"It happens!" said the sympathetic passenger. "Besides, those gauges never work accurately. The tank is empty, but the needle is far from the zero mark. It would be good to have a gas tank that would send a telepathic signal somehow when the gas is almost gone."

And suddenly the inventor appeared.

"It could be done without telepathy," he said. "I have an idea...."

What did the inventor offer?

Let us make an analysis. The automobile in our case is a supersystem. Our solution should not jeopardize any "interest" of that system. This means that nothing should be changed or redesigned in the automobile. This is typical for any supersystem as long as the problem does not require drastic changes or replacement of that system. We will consider this a requirement.

Subsystems also have their own requirements. The car's fuel control system (our central system) consists of four subsystems: gas, gas tank, something that makes a signal ("X" — what we are going to find), and the driver's head. To begin with, any "modification" of the driver's head is not acceptable. We also cannot consider any changes in the gas. There are two subsystems left: "X" and the gas tank.

Now, let's examine the condition when there is no gas in the tank — or almost none — and there is a signal from "X." Remember, the gas tank has a very simple requirement: It cannot be changed. So, the conclusion is that "X" should almost equal

32

nothing, otherwise the gas tank or the automobile must be modified. For example, "X" cannot be an X-Ray device because it would make the car more complicated.

By this time the requirements for the supersystem, the system and the subsystems have became so clear that we can determine "X" with mathematical accuracy. A little later I will show you how it can be done. Think it over yourself for now. The empty, or almost empty, gas tank should send a signal to the head of the driver. When the tank is full of gas, there is no signal. Only "X" can help us to achieve this. "X" should be so small that neither the car (the supersystem) nor the gas (the subsystem) would require any changes with its introduction.

Chapter 8
Four Periods of the System

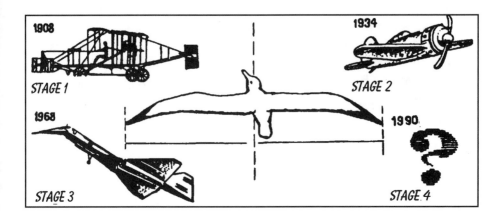

Every new system has to pass a test. A very strict jury checks out the results of this test. The jury consists of "Life" and "Practice." The jury asks: "What is it? Ah, it's an engine! Let's see how it works in the system. Well, it' is not bad. We will give it a mark of *3* (on a scale 1-5). And what is this? Ah, is this a power transmission? Yes. This transmission is very good, we will give it a *5*. Where is the control system? Is it only two buttons? What if the conditions of work are changed? What if we had an emergency? We will give this system a grade of *2*."

The rules of the jury are very simple. Only systems that do not have a mark of "2" can pass the test. It does not matter what marks the system has so long as they are not "2." The main requirement from the jury is that all subsystems should work together even if they have lower marks. It may appear strange, but all contemporary Systems at the beginning of their development had low marks. The first steamboat had a gluttonous steam engine. The transmission from the engine to the paddle-wheels devoured almost all available energy. The paddle-wheel itself did not work efficiently. Even in that form, the system had a big future because it was a very good combination. Although all the parts worked inefficiently, they did work together.

A technical System is similar to an orchestra. It is only as good as the musicians' synchronized playing. Therefore, the inventor's effort should be concentrated in the beginning on finding the best combination of a system's parts. This is the First Period in the life of a System.

There are Four Periods, and each has its own problems and methods for solutions.

Let us learn about these stages from the history of the development of the airplane.

The First Period:
Selection of Parts for the System

The development of airplanes started about one hundred years ago. Inventors were interested in determining, "What is a flying apparatus? What parts should it consist of? Should it be wings with an engine, or wings without an engine? What type of wings should be used — stationary, or flexible like a bird's wings? What kind of engine — muscles, steam, electrical or gas powered?"

Finally the airplane's formula was found. The wings were stationary and the engine was of internal combustion.

The Second Period:
Improvements of Parts

This started with the "correction of bad marks." Inventors were improving different parts of the System. They were looking for better shapes and how to optimize their relationship. They were looking for the best materials, sizes and so on. How many wings should an airplane have? Should it be a triplane, biplane or monoplane? Where should the controls be placed — in the front or in the rear? Where should the engine be placed? What kind of propellers should be designed — to pull or to push? How many gears should an airplane have? At the end of the Second Period, the airplane looked quite familiar to us.

The Third Period:
Dynamization of the System

The parts immediately began losing their own image. Parts that used to be permanently connected changed into parts having flexible connections. People invented retractable landing gear. The wings now can change their profile. The front part of the fuselage can be moved up or down. Airplanes were developed with swivel engines that produce a vertical lift. Sectional airplanes have been patented where part of the fuselage can be removed, loaded and placed back.

The Fourth Period:
Self-development of the System

This has not yet been revealed. We are just beginning to witness a few very shy steps into the fourth period — rocket and space systems. Spaceships can reorganize themselves during operation. They can get rid of rocket boosters, open solar panels while in orbit, and deliver satellites into orbit. These are only the first steps in the development of systems that can adapt themselves to a changing environment. All futuristic systems initially are seen as fantasy, but when new technologies materialize, these fantasies become reality. After all, when Jules Verne wrote his stories about space flight, they were also "just" fantasy.

Now, let's review the Four Periods:
1. Selection of parts for the System.
2. Improvements of parts.
3. Dynamization of the System.
4. Self-development of the System.

One has the right to ask: "What are we gaining by having knowledge about these periods?"

Let's look at a specific example:

A long time ago, inventors developed a device to weigh or measure different types of objects — steel balls, nails, screws and so on. The device was very simple: A funnel and a cylindrical container with two gates. The balls to be measured were loaded through the funnel into the container. When the upper gate was opened, the balls filled all the space, then the upper gate was closed and the bottom gate was opened to discharge the balls. This device was called a batcher. With this batcher, the balls are measured by volume. The volume of balls per batch equals the volume of the cylinder between two gates.

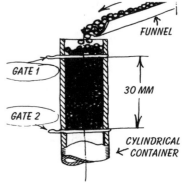

FUNNEL

GATE 1

30 MM

GATE 2

CYLINDRICAL
CONTAINER

Although this is a simple system, it is a realistic one. In 1967 this system was improved. Three inventors got the patent rights on a new batcher where the mechanical gates were replaced with electromagnetic ones. When the power is turned off for the upper magnet, the balls will fall down and fill the space between the gates. Now we can turn the upper magnet on and the lower magnet off. The measured balls will discharge from the batcher.

There is a new task now: Make an invention to improve the batcher. Without a knowledge of the laws of System Development you might be lost. Nothing in the task indicates that the magnetic batcher is bad. I am certain that you can solve this problem very easily.

This System is in the Second Period of its development. The next invention should bring this system into the Third Period.

The Third Period is Dynamization. This means that the fixed magnets should become moveable. Now, when we have to change the volume of the measured material we can simply move the upper magnet up or down along the pipe. The batching system has gained a new quality! The batcher with moveable magnets, Patent #312810, was invented five years after the magnetic gate was invented. This system could have been invented much earlier — literally the minute after the magnetic gate was invented. Five years were lost! Maybe this is not too much of a loss, but there are thousands and thousands of cases just like this! To make the system more dynamic is **Method #10: Dynamization.**

Problem 20
There is a catamaran/there is no catamaran

In the ship repairing dock a new steamboat-catamaran was built.

"It is a wonderful ship," said the old master.

"Yes, it is a beautiful ship," agreed the engineer. "The main advantage of this ship is that it is very stable. This ship will go through many different conditions — partially on rivers, partially on the ocean. It is relatively calm on rivers, but on the ocean...."

And suddenly the Inventor appears.

"This ship is indeed very wonderful, nobody will argue that," he said. "But it needs one more improvement. It should be a catamaran, and not a catamaran."

What kind of improvement do you think the Inventor had in mind?

When you work on this problem, keep in mind that the system "catamaran + river" is part of a supersystem — "river transportation." This means that the catamaran should consider the interests of all parts of the supersystem.

Now we will offer you a special problem. This problem is different from others. It is possible to come up with something new — a solution that could be an invention. In other words, this is not a textbook problem. It is a real inventive task. Do not rush the answer. Think it over, find an interesting solution, and try to develop it.

Problem 21
The law is the law

One day the president of a toy company invited his engineers to a meeting and asked them: "Can we invent a new doll based on Vanka-Vstanka?"

The engineers said that Nevalyashka [a doll weighted on the bottom so that it always returns to an upright position] and the Vanka-Vstanka were invented a long time ago. What more can we discover? This is a very simple toy. The body of the toy has a round bottom. The inside of the body is hollow and a weight is attached to the bottom inside. If you try to place the toy on its side, it will get up and swing from side to side for a while and then stand upright.

"It is really simple," said the young engineer. "Nothing could be added or removed."

"Inventor Zaitsev has invented a new Vanka-Vstanka," argued the director. "Look, Patent #645661 was issued for this new design."

The engineers bent over the new toy. On the outside, this toy looked like the previous ones. The trick was inside. The weight was mounted on a shaft in such a way that it could move along the shaft up or down. The toy could swing standing on its head or lying horizontally.

"This is the law of increasing dynamization," said the chief engineer. "In the beginning, parts of the machine had rigid connections. Later the inventors worked out flexible connections. A toy is like a machine, therefore the development of a toy should follow the same laws of development as a machine. I can predict that somebody will come up with a Vanka-Vstanka where the weight is divided and will make these parts moveable," he said.

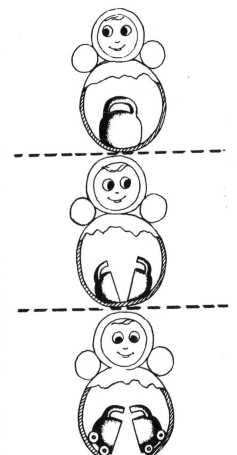

"It is already figured out," said the president of the company. "This is the "Vanka-Vstanka" invented by the inventor Litvinenko. Patent #676290."

He placed on the table one more toy of the Vanka-Vstanka series. The doll was swinging differently, the swinging frequency was changing all the time.

"That's it," said the chief engineer while opening the body of the toy. "The weight is divided, the parts have become moveable in the same way as in an hourglass. The sand is moving from one portion of the glass into the other, changing the weight of each portion. Therefore the frequency changes."

"Everything new that has been done, was done in another factory!" exclaimed the president. "Are they better than we are? Couldn't we think of something else? You said that there is the Law of Increasing Dynamization. Very well, let's use this law and invent another Vanka-Vstanka that will be more dynamic."

And suddenly the Inventor appeared.

"The Law is the Law," he said. "There is a way to make this toy more dynamic. I would like to offer...."

What can you suggest?

Chapter 9
M-Field From Generation of S-Field

Now we would like to offer you a more difficult problem. By the way, you already have seen that a difficult problem is difficult only because we do not know the Laws of Development of technical systems.

Problem 22
The universal field

At a factory that makes agricultural machinery, there is a small piece of fenced land that is used for testing equipment mobility. Once, the factory got orders to manufacture machinery for many different countries. Those different countries have different soils. The factory found that in order to test all those machines it would need many different soil compositions.

"We need 140 different fields," said the president of the factory to his engineer at the meeting. "How can we get so much land?"

"It will take a lot of money as well," added the chief accountant. "No, it is not realistic to build 140 fields! The situation is hopeless!"

And suddenly the Inventor appeared.

"There are no hopeless situations," he said. "We can build one universal field that would replace 140. What we need is...."

What do you think we need?

A detailed explanation follows.

I hope that you won't offer as a solution any of the following:

a. Divide the main field into 140 pieces. The factory field is not big.

b. Deliver machines to all the different countries. Every machine has to be tested many times, and the expense would be tremendous.

c. Change the soil on the field the way it is done in the circus (140 moveable areas).

d. Freeze and defrost the soil (this is too slow).

e. Deliver different types of soil (too slow and expensive).

Such ideas would improve only one thing and worsen another. We have to overcome the technical contradiction in order to change the quality of the soil without making it unacceptably complicated, expensive, or by increasing the size of the field.

Let's first set the conditions of the task. What is given? The soil is a Substance that we will designate with the symbol S_1. It is necessary to learn to control the parameters of S_1 by employing some "field" force. Let us designate this field force with the letter F. Now we can draw a diagram:

There are six basic fields:

1. Gravitational: F_{GR}

2. Electromagnetic (electrical/ magnetic): F_E / F_{MG}

3. Nuclear field of weak interaction: F_{NW}

4. Nuclear field of strong interaction: F_{NS}

5. Mechanical: F_M

6. Thermal: F_T

We will not consider the nuclear fields. What we need is a very simple solution. We have to eliminate the gravitational field as well because we have not yet learned how to control it.

There are three fields left — electromagnetic, mechanical, and thermal. Now we can understand why this task is a difficult one. Soil does not react to an electromagnetic force, and is very reluctant to respond to mechanical and thermal fields. We can clearly see a physical contradiction. Field F should act on substance S_1 (soil) — this is by the specifications of the problem — but field F cannot act on this substance because the fields we are using have no effect on the parameters of substance S_1.

This type of contradiction can be found in many tasks. There is one typical method that could be used to remove this type of contradiction. If it is impossible for field F to act directly on substance S_1, then a *bypass* way should be implemented. Let field F act on substance S_1 *through another substance, S_2, that has a good response to field F.*

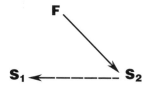

There is an action (indirect), and there is no action (direct).

Suppose we decide to use a magnetic field. What kind of a substance should S_2 be? The answer is obvious. A ferromagnetic substance should be used. For instance, iron powder is a good substance because it could be mixed easily with substance S_1 (soil). Magnetized particles are attracted to each other. The stronger the magnetic field, the stronger the attractive power. A mixture of soil with ferromagnetic powder in a strong magnetic field could be as strong as granite. The same mixture in a weak magnetic field could be as soft as sand.

Hence, if the iron powder is mixed with some substance, a magnetic field could easily control the property of that substance — compress, stretch, bend, relocate and so on.

This is Method #11: Add magnetic powder to the substance and apply a magnetic field.

This combination has exceptional power. Here are several examples:

Oil tankers occasionally dump water polluted with oil into the ocean. This is usually punished by high fines. The problem is to prove that the oil on the ocean surface belongs to a particular tanker. Recently, a very smart method was offered. During the loading process a small amount of fine magnetic particles (for each tanker those particles have their own characteristics) was added to the oil. When the Coast Guard finds an oil spot on the ocean surface, a sample is taken, and the analysis of the magnetic particles will indicate to which tanker it belongs.

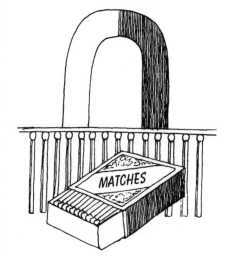

Another example: During the process of manufacturing particle boards it is desirable to have elongated wooden chips positioned along the length of the board. This will increase the strength of the board. How is this done? It is impossible to place every chip by hand. An inventor suggested the use of magnetic powder. The particles of that powder will strongly adhere to every chip, and a magnet will arrange the chips the way we need them.

It is possible to force magnetic powder to adhere to cotton fiber. This will simplify the process of spinning the cotton. Later the particles can be washed away without damaging the quality of the fabric.

One more example: If magnetic particles were added to the mixture from which wooden match-heads are made, we will get magnetic matches that are easier to package. In general, adding magnetic particles to any object simplifies automation of the packaging process.

The next problem is a very easy one for you to try. Strictly speaking, this problem is not easier than the problem about "testing machinery." But with new knowledge, you should be able to solve this problem without any difficulties

Problem 23
Wait, Rabbit, I will get you!

To make a cartoon movie, it is necessary to make thousands of drawings. In every yard of movie film there are about 52 drawings. In a ten minute movie there are more than 15,000 drawings! One movie-studio decided to make a "contour" film. This is how it was done. On a flat surface the artist lays out a picture with colored string. The operator takes a shot, the artist moves the string, and the operator again takes another shot, and so on. It is easier to move the string than to draw a new picture.

"That is too slow," said the operator.

"Yes, you are right, it is slow," said the artist making the corrections to the string. "In order to make a rabbit run across the screen, we spend a whole working day."

And suddenly the Inventor appears.

"Wait, Rabbit, I will get you," he said decisively.

What do you think the Inventor offered?

A **Triumvirate**, which includes a substance, a ferromagnetic powder and a magnetic field, is called an M-Field. The same "Triumvirate" could be built with other fields. Do you remember **Problem #15** about the stubborn spring? Probably, you have already figured out that the spring should be "hidden" in the ice. For that purpose the "Triumvirate" should be built out of a Thermal field (F_T), spring (S_1), and ice (S_2).

To have direct control over the spring is not practical in this particular problem. The best control over the spring is to use ice (preferably dry ice, because it does not produce water when heated).

In **Problem #9**, the enlargement of the droplets of the liquid substance, there is only one substance that is known — droplets. We can say at once: To solve this problem we need one more substance and a field. To simplify the task we can add ferromagnetic particles to the liquid, and control the process of "adherence" of droplets by the magnetic M-field.

It will look like this:

42

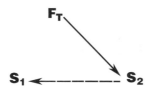

What if the specifications of the problem do not allow us to add foreign substances?

Then we have a contradiction: The second substance should be, and the second substance should not be. In this case we will divide the flow of the droplets into two parts. One drop will be charged positive, the other drop will be negative. The contradiction is removed. We have one substance, with no additives, and at the same time we have two different substances (positive, S1, and negative, S_2). The system is constructed out of two substances and a field, and the problem is solved. The droplets with different charges will adhere to each other. It is very easy to control this system by increasing and decreasing the amount of charge to the droplets.

Triumvirates with different fields (not only magnetic) are conditionally called S-Fields (from the word "substance" and "field"). Thus M-field is one part of the S-Field family, in the same way that a right-angle triangle is a part of the triangle family.

It is not a coincidence that I am comparing triangles with S-Fields. The introduction of S-Fields plays a very important role in the theory of solving inventive problems. It is the same as the value of the triangle in mathematics. The triangle is a minimal geometric figure. Any complex geometric figure could be broken down into simple triangles. If we learn to solve simple problems by using S-Fields, we can solve other more complex technical problems.

Chapter 10
The Alphabet of S-Field Analysis

S-Field formulas can be compared to chemical formulas. For example, here is the "reaction" that describes the answer to Problem 22:

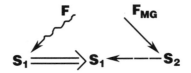

The wavy arrow means "unsatisfied action." The double arrow means "has to make a transition to another system." The broken arrow means "has to introduce an action."

The construction and transformation of the **S-Field** is a large part of the Theory of Inventive Problem Solving, and is called **"S-Field Analysis."**

At this time it is enough to just know a few simple rules:

Rule #1: In order to solve a problem that has a partial S-Field, the S-Field must be completed. This is Method #12: S-Field Analysis.

Let us now return to **Problem 19, the gas tank.** There is a substance S_1 (an empty gas tank) that does not know how to signal its own condition. By using the first rule we could easily draw a diagram of the solution to our problem:

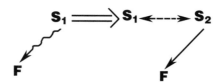

$$S_1 \Longrightarrow S_1 \leftarrow\!-\!-\!\rightarrow S_2$$

F   F

The fields acting on the substances will be drawn above the line. The fields created by the substances will be drawn below the line.

Hence, in the S-Field diagram this problem is solved. What's left is to determine S_2 and F. The field should act on the driver in our problem. This means that it could be electromagnetic, optical, mechanical, audio or thermal. The optical field is not convenient because additional optical signals will distract the driver's attention. It is even less convenient to use thermal signals. What about acoustical (sound) signals? Now we understand the role of S_2.

This substance, when the tank is empty, should interact with the tank and produce an audio signal. The problem is solved. Let us drop a simple buoy into the tank. When the tank is full of gas, the buoy floats in "silence." The sides of the buoy should have a soft surface to prevent it from making a sound when hitting the sides or top of the tank.

As soon as the tank is almost empty, the buoy will hit bottom and produce a sound that can be heard by the driver. This S-Field system we have built may be drawn as a rhombus:

$$
\begin{array}{ccc}
 & F_1 & \\
 & \searrow & \\
S_1 \leftarrow\!-\!-\!-\!-\!-\!\rightarrow & & S_2 \\
 & \swarrow & \\
 & F_2 &
\end{array}
$$

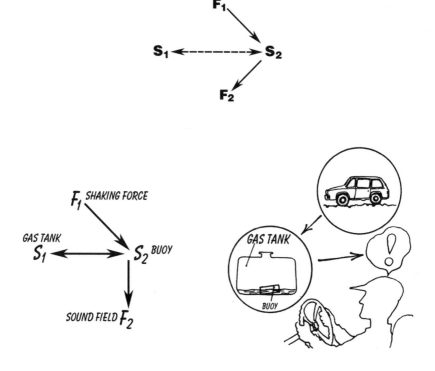

45

Or, more precisely:

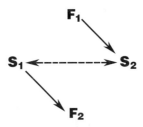

The mechanical field F_1, the energy of shaking, acts on buoy S_2, which in turn interacts with tank S_1, and thanks to that, audio field F_2 is developed.

Many problems seeking a solution in the area of measurement and detection can be solved by adding to substance S_1 a special S-Field "attachment."

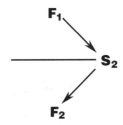

The same way as the chemical group *COOH* "attaches" to radical *R* in the organic acid formula:

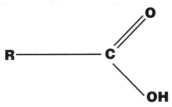

R can be different, but every organic acid, as we know, contains the group *COOH*.

Rule #2: If, by specification of the problem, a "worthless" S-Field is present, an introduction of substance S_3 between S_1 and S_2 is necessary in order to improve it. This S_3 could be a modification of S_1 or S_2. It can be shown like this:

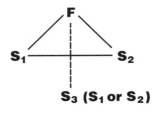

46

The S-Field can be broken down using different methods:

a. Change F, S_1, or S_2;

b. Remove F, S_1, or S_2;

c. Introduce a second field F_2, or
   substance S_3.

In order to solve the problem it is easier to introduce S_3. When this is prohibited by the conditions of the task, a contradiction arises: It is necessary to introduce a third substance S_3, and it is prohibited to do so. The following rule shows a bypass way to do that:

The third substance, S3, should be a modification of an already known substance, S_1 or S_2. Then the contradiction is removed. There is an S_3, and there is no S_3.

Let us explain this rule with an example.

Many electric power stations operate on coal. The coal is delivered by railroad cars and unloaded into large silos — reinforced concrete funnels. There is a screw conveyor similar to those found in old meat grinders. These conveyors are not used to chop the coal but only to convey it to the pipeline. Then the coal moves down the inclined pipeline by itself to the ball mill, a huge rotating cylinder with many heavy steel balls inside. The ball mill crushes the coal into crumbs and powder. A fast stream of air takes the crushed coal and brings it into a separator, where the fine powder goes into the main burners of the station, and the rest returns for another cycle of crushing. The system works well as long as dry coal comes into the system. Often, wet coal comes into the system and the "agony" begins. Wet coal sticks to the screws of the conveyor, walls of the pipe, and neck at the entrance of the mill. Later, the excess water is removed, but not before the wet coal has caused a lot of trouble.

Many inventors in different countries have tried to outwit the wet coal. They have dried it, changed the shape of the pipes, and even shaken the pipes. Fine coal is a very dangerous substance. During experiments, it can self-ignite. Fires and explosions have occurred.

Finally, Americans invented a new lining material — "polyfluoroethylene" (Teflon) to cover the inner walls of the pipes. It was very expensive, but it seemed that the problem was solved. However, it was soon learned that Teflon wears out rapidly under these conditions.

The sentence "wet coal sticks to the walls of the pipe" in the language of S-Field analysis looks like this: "The useless S-Field is given — two substances (S_1, S_2) and a mechanical field of adherence." Teflon (S_3) is a completely alien substance. The rule is broken! As you already have figured out, S_3 should not be made out of Teflon but from modified pipe metal or modified wet coal. The *wet* coal, S_1, being modified, becomes *dry* coal. This means that the role of S_3 would be played by dry coal. Even a thin layer of dry coal between the walls of the pipe and the wet coal immediately prevents adherence. When a cook is preparing raw cutlets to fry, crumbs are spread over them to prevent adherence to the frying pan. The cook uses the rule of S-Field analysis without knowing it.

Some of the dried coal powder is diverted into the screw conveyor. This is the simplest change, but the problem is solved brilliantly!

Notice that the problems about the droplets and the wet coal have some similarities; hence, in the first problem we have to build an S-Field, and in the second problem we have to destroy the S-Field.

In both problems it is required to introduce a new substance, and at the same time it is impossible — or difficult — to introduce it. This contradiction could be removed by utilizing the existing substance S_2 which, when modified, becomes S_3.

A paradoxical situation emerges. There *is no* new substance (we have used an existing one), and there *is* a new substance (we changed the existing one).

Conventional thinking uses a simple logic: "Yes" means "yes" and "no" means "no." "Black" is "black," and "white" is "white," and so on.

The Inventive Problem Solving theory develops other kinds of thinking based on dialectical logic. "Yes" and "no" can coexist: **"Yes can be no" and "black can be white."**

```
NONO        NONO        NONONONONO          NONO
NONO        NONO        NONONONONO      NONONONONO
 NONO       NONO        NONO            NONO        NONO
  NONO     NONO         NONO            NONO
     NONONONO           NONONONONO      NONON
      NONONON           NONONONONO        NONONO
       NONONO           NONO                NONONO
        NONON           NONO                  NONONO
         NONO           NONO            NONO        NONO
   NONONONONO           NONONONONO      NONONONONO
   NONONONONO           NONONONONO          NONO
```

Chapter 11
Try it Yourself

Let's recall some of the methods that we have learned so far in this part:

(6) Conflicting requirements are separated in time or space.

(7) All special terms must be replaced with simple words.

(8) Incorporation of similar or different objects into one system.

(9) Fragmentation / Consolidation.

(10) Dynamization.

(11) Add magnetic powder to a substance and then apply a magnetic field.

(12) S-Field Analysis.

Now, let's do some exercises.

Here are several problems. Remember, during the process of solving problems you have to use the methods and rules that you have learned. You must drop the habit of looking for a solution blindly, or by rule of thumb, picking up different variants.

Problem 24
In spite of all storms

In the ocean, not far from the beach, a hydraulic dredge was working. It made channels deeper for bigger ships. The ground lifted from the bottom of the ocean was mixed with the ocean water, and pumped through a pipeline five kilometers long. This long tail of pipes was floating on the waves behind the dredge. Empty metal barrel-pontoons were keeping the pipes afloat.

"There is a weather forecast about a severe storm coming in," said the foreman of the shift. "We have to stop working, disconnect the tail, and bring it into the bay. After the storm we will bring it back and connect it. We may lose all day doing this."

"What can we do?" the mechanic asked. "If the storm breaks the pipeline, it will be much worse."

And here the Inventor appeared.

"We can work in spite of all storms," he said. "The system "pipe-pontoon" should become...."

What kind of system is he talking about, and how should it work?

Problem 25
Propeller for Carlson

The director of a large toy store came to a toy factory and said to the chief engineer, "our customers are asking for a toy — a flying doll called Carlson — but we do not have it in our store. We see tears in the eyes of children every day. Help us!"

"We have two samples of a toy called Carlson," answered the engineer. "Take a look...."

One doll was a close copy of the original Carlson, but it couldn't fly. The other had a propeller much bigger than the Carlson doll itself. This doll couldn't stand-up — but it could fly like a toy helicopter.

"It's too bad," said the director. "One doll looks like Carlson, but cannot fly. The other doll can fly but does not look like Carlson — it looks like a windmill."

"This is a technical contradiction," the engineer said spreading his arms. "To make a small propeller is no good — Carlson will not fly, there is not enough power from the small propeller. If we make the propeller bigger we will destroy the appearance of the doll, and it will not stand by itself. I really do not know what to do."

And here, of course, the Inventor appeared.

"Let's start from the physical contradiction," he said. "The prop should be big and should not be big. Everything is clear, we should use the method...."

What method is he talking about, and how can he use it?

Problem 26
Ten thousand pyramids

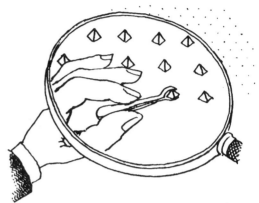

In a research laboratory people were trying to develop diamond tools for polishing surfaces. The tools came out very well, but it was difficult to manufacture them. The diamond grains had a pyramid shape and were very small. It was necessary to place them on the surface of the tool by hand, with their tips facing up.

"Ten thousand pyramids, and all by hand," said the agitated workers. "Why can't someone think of some way to mechanize this work?"

"We have tried," answered the supervisor of the lab, "but nothing good has emerged."

And here the Inventor appeared.

"It is a wonderful problem," he said. "We have to recall the method...."

What method must we recall? How can the placement of the diamonds be mechanized?

Problem 27
An almost excellent machine

At the industrial agricultural show an engineer was giving a demonstration of a fruit packaging conveyor.

Before this conveyor, fruits were packaged into carton containers by hand. Now, it is done by machine. The conveyor places the container on the table. The fruits roll down through a trough. An electric motor vibrates the table for the fruits to be packed properly. This is an excellent machine, but it has one defect. When the fruits fall into the container they hit each other and are damaged.

"Is it possible to lower the trough along which the fruit slides down to the container?" asked one of the visitors.

"Yes, this is possible," said the engineer. "The problem now is that while you are filling the container up you have to lift the trough. This means that we need an automatic system to control it. The machine will become more complicated. To lower the container is even more complicated...."

And suddenly the Inventor appeared.

"One apple hits the other one," he said. "This is a task for the rule of *destroying the S-Field*. Take...."

And he explained how to fix it so that none of the fruits will be damaged during the fall, even the most fragile ones.

What can you offer?

Problem 28
There is no fountain like that

The authorities of a certain town decided to build a fountain. A competition was announced. The Committee looked through the designs that were submitted by the architects.

"There is nothing exciting. All this has already been built," said the jury sadly. "We would like to have a fountain that would be the only one of its kind in the whole world."

"Can you think of something better?" asked one of the members of the jury. "People have been building fountains for a long time. The principle is the same — streams of water crossing each other. In one of the projects an architect offered to use a light inside the fountain. This is not new either! There are fountains with fire, light — even with color and music."

And suddenly the Inventor appeared.

"I am going to offer a fountain design that nobody has built yet. It is going to be the most beautiful and surprising spectacle!"

Try to figure out what the Inventor offered. Maybe you can continue developing his idea and create a new invention.

Part 3
The Science of Inventing

Chapter 12
Cunning and Physics

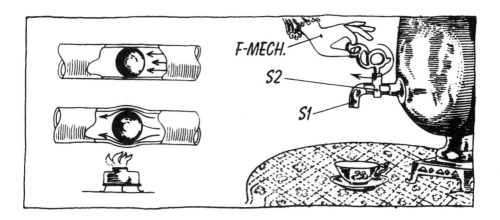

By this time, you have already read one third of this book. Let's summarize everything you have read so far:

Long ago, inventive problems were worked out — and even now in the majority of cases — by using the **"Trial and Error"** method. This method, however, is often ineffective. It takes a lot of time, effort, and resources. Often inventions were created many years later.

The scientific-technical revolution requires a completely new method for solving technical problems. To this end, The **Theory for Solving Inventive Problems (TRIZ)** was created. It teaches us to solve problems without selecting an "empty" traditional variant. Here is the basic idea: The evolution of a technical system, like any other system, is subject to the general laws of evolution. The knowledge of these laws allows you to develop the methods and tools for solving inventive tasks.

There are three groups of methods that you have learned so far:

1. Various tricks (i.e., **Do it in advance**).

2. The methods based on utilizing physical effects and phenomena. (i.e., **Changing the state of physical properties of substances**).

3. Complex methods that include tricks and physics. (i.e., **Building F-Fields**).

Very often, during the problem solving process, one uses a trick first, and then physics. Success comes with applying both methods. Therefore, the application of physics during the problem solving process is one of the major areas in the Theory of Inventiveness.

Let's see how a combination of tricks and physics works.

Problem 29
It is going to work forever!

In a certain plant, one robot kept breaking down. It was a very good robot, but one simple part kept breaking. It was a bent pipe through which compressed air carried steel balls at high speed. The balls would hit the inner wall of the pipe in an area of the bend. Every time a ball hit the wall, a small piece of metal chipped off. After a couple of working hours, this particular section of the pipe wore out completely, creating a hole in the thick, rugged pipe.

Let's install two pipes," said the supervisor. "While one is working, we will have time to repair the other one."

And suddenly the Inventor appears.

"What good is it to keep repairing the pipe?" he exclaimed. "I have a very suitable idea. I will guarantee that this machine will work forever!"

It took only five minutes to put this idea into practice. What did he offer?

Let's make an S-Field analysis.

There is one substance S_1 (steel balls) that mechanically interacts with the other substance S_2 (pipe wall). Therefore, a useless (even harmful) S-Field exists. Someone at the plant tried to destroy this S-Field by introducing a third substance S_3 — different linings and layers. This is the wrong approach. The correct way is to use a third substance S_3 to protect the wall so that it will not be destroyed by the steel balls. This substance could be the same steel balls, placed along the curve of the inner side of the pipe.

In this case the wall would be protected by a layer of balls. Flying balls could knock off one or two balls from the protective layer, but they would be replaced immediately by other balls flying in the pipe. This is the essence of the trick. **This is Method #13: Self-Service.**

Now we need to know some of the physical laws on how to use **Self-Service**. In order to develop the protective layer of the balls, we need to use a magnet. We will place the magnet on the outside of the bend. Some of the balls from the flow will stick to the wall inside the pipe as soon as they reach the magnetized area. The problem is solved! We should mention that pellet blasting guns were known long before this. These guns were used to harden the surface of steel about a quarter of a century before Patent #261207 on magnetic protection was issued. Everybody saw the

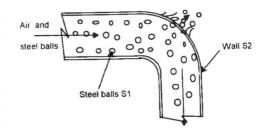

problem but they were trying to solve it contrary to the Theory by using linings, or by making that part of the pipe from stronger and harder steel.

Problem 30
Super precision valve

The manager of a chemical laboratory invited an inventor and said: "We have to control the gas flow through this metal pipe that connects these two containers. The gas flow is controlled by valves with polished glass stems. This type of valve cannot guarantee the required accuracy of the gas flow — it is difficult to adjust the size of the opening through which the gas flows."

"Of course," said the inventor. "It is like the valve on a Russian tea samovar."

The chemist behaved as if he did not hear anything. "We can," continued the chemist, "install a rubber hose and a clip. But even that will not give us the required accuracy."

"Clips," laughed the Inventor. "Clothespins...."

The chemist suddenly blew up. "We have been working like that for hundreds of years. Try to think of the valve as a simple "clip" or samovar valve but with an accuracy that is ten times higher."

And suddenly the Inventor replied.

"It takes a little bit of cunning plus tenth grade physics. What we have to do is ...." What did the Inventor offer?

For a person experienced in TRIZ, the valve is a typical S-Field system. The body of the valve is S_1, the turning stem is S_2, the mechanical field is F_M. The mechanical field Fm moves part S_2, hence the clearance between S_1 and S_2 becomes bigger or smaller. The S-Field already exists, but works unsatisfactorily. This means that we have to build another S-Field with a different F. What kind of Field could we use — electrical, magnetic, electromagnetic, thermal?

Here is where the trick ends and physics starts. In the physics textbook there is a chapter about the expansion of a substance when heat is applied. This is what we are looking for: Change the size of the gap between S_1 and S_2. **This is Method #14: Heat expansion.**

Let us open the physics textbook. This is the description of the experiment: "The ball that could not go through a cold ring can now go through a heated one..." And below are the drawings of the ball and the ring. This is the model for our valve.

Let's compare this solution with Patent #179489. A device to control the rate of gas flow comprising a valve body and a stem that sits tight inside the body. In order to control the rate of the gas flow with the highest accuracy, the valve body should be made out of a material with a high coefficient of expansion and the stem should be made out of material with a low coefficient of expansion. You have probably already figured out how that valve works. As soon as heat is applied, the body of the valve will expand more than the stem, creating a space between the body and the stem. The more heat is applied the more clearance is created. The significance of the invention is that, instead of using many big moveable parts, a crystal structure for the valve components is used.

By the way, the expansion and contraction of the crystal grid could be done not only by a thermal field. For instance, some quartz crystals — Seignette salt and Tourmaline — will change their crystal grids in an electrical field. This is from a twelfth grade physics textbook, and is called the "Reverse Piezoeffect." You have probably figured out that the same effect could be used to develop a micro-valve. There is one more similar effect — "Magnetostriction." A magnetic field could expand or contract some metal materials. This is another answer to the problem of the valve.

Problem 31
Let's look into the future

If one wants to get the residue of toothpaste from an almost empty tube, one can place the tube on a hard surface and squeeze it with a pencil. This is the same principle as that used in a peristaltic pump. The rollers press the flexible hose against the body of the pump, and by moving the roller along the wall, the liquid or paste is forced to flow through the hose.

"We manufacture twenty types of this pump," said the chief engineer to his assistant. "In the next month we will bring three more to the market. But, even though in principle all these pumps are the same, they differ in size and application. Is this how pumps will look in the future?"

"Probably they will not change," said the assistant. "The principle is the same, isn't it?"

And here, Inventors appeared — three of them!

"Of course new pumps will be developed," confirmed the first Inventor.

"The peristaltic principle would be preserved, but the action would be transferred to the micro level," said the second.

"We are offering to use physical effects," said the third. "We will have three new peristaltic pumps."

The Inventors started to open their drawings.

What is your opinion about how these pumps should work? What type of physical effects could be used?

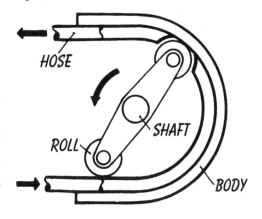

Chapter 13
How to Solve Problems
that do not Exist Yet

The transition from the "rough" movement of "metal parts" to the fine movement of molecules and atoms is another principle of technical evolution. Therefore the method for solving many tasks is **Method #15: Transition from macrostructure to microstructure.**

An example of this method is Patent #438327. In this patent the vibro-gyroscope is oscillated by outside alternating electrical fields and has electrons and charged ions as a vibrating mass.

Massive weights mounted on rods was the conventional design of the vibro-gyroscope. The principle of the invention is that microparticles (electrons and ions) are used instead of massive weights. This type of gyro requires less space and works much more accurately.

In the previous chapter, you have read about the four periods of the development of technical systems. You probably have asked yourself, "Okay, the systems go through four periods, but what is next?"

There are two possibilities that I have already talked about. When the system reaches its own limits it **joins** another system and a **new, more complex system emerges**. Thus the development continues. For example, the bicycle combined with the internal combustion engine and became a motor-cycle. As a new system evolves, the development continues.

Sometimes the road to consolidation between systems is closed. It is necessary to consolidate systems and yet it is impossible to do so. This type of contradiction could be removed by **breaking up the existing system and recombining its parts into a new system.** Restrictions were mainly related to unification with foreign systems, and we did not break these restrictions.

What if it is forbidden to consolidate or to break up systems? Suppose that we have a task. We need to increase the springiness of a spiral spring without adding anything to it or breaking it up. Consider that the most appropriate material for the spring has been chosen, and changing that material will not make sense.

At first glance, the situation seems hopeless. Nothing can be changed. How do we make a transition to a new system? And yet, there is a solution! The new system is "hidden" inside the old one. We usually look at the spring as a piece of "iron," but inside of that piece of "iron" are whole worlds of particles. A gigantic system exists — and does not exist because we are not using it! Let's magnetize the spring in such a way that over each loop a similar magnetic pole would be developed. The similar charges will repel each other and, therefore, compression of the spring will require more energy. The problem is solved. The spring looks as though nothing has changed. We did not add anything or breakup anything.

Conclusion:

There are **two directions** for the development of systems that seem to have used-up all their resources of development.

The first direction is the consolidation of the existing system with other systems, or the fragmentation of subsystems and their subsequent recombination into a new system.

The second direction is the transition from macrostructure (macrolevel) to microstructure (microlevel) where the internal world of the system — particles, molecules and atoms — are involved.

Here I would like to offer you an invention: Patent #489662. This is a device for applying a polymer powder. This device is comprised of a compartment and an electrode. In order to increase the quality of the applied layer of powder, the electrode has a microscrew that allows the electrode to travel. Originally, the electrode had a firm connection to the compartment. The inventor offered to make this electrode moveable. **This is a transition of the system from the second stage of its development to the third stage.** You already know these transitions.

Being familiar with the laws of technical system evolution, we can predict the future development of the system. This means that the system now should go from **the third stage to the fourth.** It should become not just adjustable (flexible) but **self-adjustable.** The electrode should move by itself relative to the changes in the environment. **The final transition of the system is when the control is made on microlevels.** This means that instead of a screw to adjust the position of the rod, a thermal field could be used, or a piezoeffect, or magnetostriction.

Remember that we are investigating answers to problems that have not appeared yet! Years will pass by, and life will require increased accuracy in this process. Only then will the problem appear — the problem we have already solved.

When the method of trial and error is used, the answer to a problem usually appears *much* later. The Theory of Inventing changes this situation — we understand the logic of technical systems evolution and can foresee the arising of new problems, knowing beforehand how they can be solved.

Chapter 14
"Crown" Performance of the Corona Discharge

In textbooks of physics, the effects and phenomenon described are very "neutral." Any matter will expand when heat is applied. That's it. What if the same effects could be described in an "inventive" manner? For instance: **The substance will expand when heat is applied; therefore, this phenomenon could be used in all cases when we need to control very small and precise movements**. If we rewrite all the textbooks of physics, we will get a very powerful tool, a catalog of physical effects and phenomenon

Let's take, for instance, the description of the phenomenon called the "Corona Discharge" described in an eleventh grade physics textbook. One can observe the discharge in heterogeneous (nonuniform) electrical fields at regular atmospheric pressure. This discharge emits a light in the shape of a "crown," therefore it was called the "Corona Discharge." The density of the charge on the surface of the conductor is relative to its curvature — the more curvature, the greater the charge. The maximum density of the charge is at the sharp edge of the conductor, where the strongest electrical field is developed. When the voltage of the field exceeds 3×10^6 V/m the discharge strikes. Ionization under this condition will appear during normal atmospheric pressure. The voltage charge weakens with the increase of distance from the conductor. Therefore, the ionization and emission of light is limited in space. We have to be very careful with the "Corona Discharge" because of its high voltage. The "Corona Discharge" could start with the presence of thin conductors or parts projecting outside.

61

Thus, the presence of the "corona" depends on the composition of the gas as well as its pressure surrounding the conductor.

This is Method #16: Effects of the Corona discharge.

The Corona discharge will help us to solve **Problem #1** about the measurement of gas pressure inside the light bulb. If we apply high voltage to the spiral element of the bulb, the formation of the Corona Discharge will occur. The brightness of the "Crown" will depend on the pressure of the gas inside the bulb.

Let's go back to the textbook. The Corona Discharge produces ionized gas. If particles of powder, dust, or small droplets are present in the gas, the ions will "stick" to them. Therefore, the Corona discharge will charge those particles of solid and liquid substances. Now, it is easy to control these particles. The "Corona" could be used to clean gases from dust, to disperse particles suspended in a gas flow, to transport different powders, to determine the additives in gases, and so on.

Producing charged particles is the main "crown performance" of the Corona Discharge. As you can see, the simplest physical phenomenon conceals the richest potential for inventiveness.

Chapter 15
What Was the Boss Thinking About?

So far we have talked about simple physical effects that everybody in school knows. However, there is a more complicated physics — the physics that college students learn. The knowledge of this physics gives an inventor more powerful tools.

This time, we will study a problem that requires only the knowledge of elementary physics. Later I will explain what we can achieve if we use just a little physics from college.

Problem 32
Ice on the electric power lines

It was a beautiful view — the electric wires were covered with fluffy snow. For the electricians, this beauty does not provoke excitement. When the snow melts, it turns to ice. The layers of ice grow, and the wires will stretch and break under the heavy weight of the ice.

In a small northern town an electric power station was working. This station was about 100 km away from the town. It was a normal procedure in the winter time to heat the electric lines. A strong current was applied, the wires were heated, and the ice melted from the lines. During that time, all the customers were disconnected. It was a very cold winter, and the director of the station began to worry about the heavy icing. He gave instructions to heat the lines more often, which meant that the customers would be disconnected more often. The factories were stopped and the lights in the houses were shut off. The customers complained, and the director decided to heat the lines less often. The wires started to break, and the town was left without power more often.

"What should we do?" the director was thinking as he looked at the calendar. There are many more months of northern winter ahead.

"This is a technical contradiction. If we heat the lines more often the customers will complain. If we heat them less frequently, the danger of breaking will occur. This is a nightmare."

And suddenly the Inventor appeared.

"Let us open the physics textbook for the eighth grade," he said. "We have to finish building the S-Field diagram and then we will use the effect of electromagnetic induction."

Why did the inventor remind us to finish building the S-Field? How do we use electromagnetic induction?

There is an electric line (substance S_1) and an electric current (field F_E). Ice is prohibited on the line. This means that we have only the substance and the field. In order to have an S-Field, we have to bring in the second substance S_2. This second substance under regular electric current will heat itself and heat the line. What is the trick here? The wire of the electric line is made of material with very low resistance, and it does not warm up under the existing current. Wire with a high resistance will warm up, but the customers will not get electricity. This is a physical contradiction. The resistance of the wire should be high and it should not be high. The inventor offered to add a second substance. The wire remains the same, but every five meters a ferrite ring will be installed over the wire. This ring has a very high electric resistance. The electric current is developed in the rings by electromagnetic induction. The rings will warm up very fast and will radiate heat to the wires.

The patent was issued on that principle, but this problem could have been solved by school children who have learned the basics of S-Field analysis.

It seems like the problem is solved. A good answer has been reached. However, the ferrite rings heat the line all year round. You can imagine how much energy will be wasted! Even in the winter time, it is not necessary to warm up all the lines. Only those parts of the line that are in areas where the temperatures goes below 32^0 F actually need warming. A new task appears: How to turn the rings on when there are low temperatures and turn them off during high temperatures?

In order to work on that problem one should know that ferrite rings will remain ferromagnetic only up to a certain temperature level called the Curie point. Different ferromagnetic materials have different Curie points. It is possible to make a ferromagnetic material with a Curie point of about 32^0 F. This means that those rings would turn on only when the temperature drops below 32^0 F, and turn off when the temperature is above 32^0 F.

Appearance and disappearance of the magnetic characteristics during the transition through the Curie points could be used to solve many other inventive problems. Remember this very interesting physical phenomenon.

This is Method #17: Curie point of ferromagnetic materials.

Chapter 16
The Immense Science of Physics

Anry Grijoh, a patient in a mental hospital, was in an inventive mood. He was trying to invent solid water that would not melt at temperatures below 200^0 C. This is what happened:

In the imaginary story "The Insane" by Polish writer Stephen Vainfel, Grijoh got some white granulated powder. Under high heat, the powder becomes clear water.

The story was published in 1964. In 1967, three years later, solid water was invented. This water consisted of 90% water and 10% silicic acid. The solid water looked like white powder.

The question may arise: Why do we need solid water?

Let us see what Andri Grijoh would say:

"My invention allows us to build factories in areas that are rich in natural resources, but poor in water. If today water is delivered in trailer tanks, tomorrow water will be delivered in paper bags. What will happen to trade? All kinds of metal, glass and ceramic containers used to transport liquid would disappear completely. Liquid will be sold in powder form.

"There are thousands — tens of thousands — of ways of using dry water. In our everyday life it would bring about a technical revolution. To use water in liquid form would become as ridiculous as using chipped wood as a source of light."

Scientists are trying to develop a solid water that will only contain two-three percent silicic acid. There is nothing mentioned about this in physics books as yet. Physics is developing very fast, and all the time new effects and phenomena are being discovered. You can imagine how important it is for inventors to know about the latest developments.

Here is a typical story: While one group of scientists was trying to develop solid water, another group of scientists was working to make water more liquid. In 1948, the English scientist B. Thomas discovered a very surprising physical effect. The friction of water inside pipes could be reduced by using minute amounts (1/100 percent) of some polymers. Friction usually occurs because of the turbulence developed in the fast flow. Long molecules of polymers in the water position themselves along the flow, reduce the vortices, and make the water more slippery.

The result of the Thomas discovery was published, and soon many inventions appeared, that used this effect. The Thomas effect helped to increase the speed of ships, to lower the energy consumption during transportation of different liquids through pipes, and to increase the distance of water shooting from a firehose nozzle. Recently, inventors from Moscow University offered to add polymers to the ice in skating arenas. Thanks to this invention, the high pressure under the skate blade melts the ice more readily. The polymer added to the water reduces the friction of skating.

We can give you many similar examples. The inventor needs to know the immense science of physics — thousands and thousands of effects. You can say that there are no physicists who know all the aspects of physics. It is not necessary for the inventors to know physics better than the physicists do. The answer lies in making a reference book that will include physical effects and phenomena for the inventor's application. It would be similar to the "Corona" effect, but the description should be more complete and accurate. The very first such reference book was published in the beginning of 1970. In these books, the physical effects were stated in the light of inventive use. It seems that another reference book should be compiled with different combinations of physical effects. This has not yet been done, probably, because the number of combinations is huge.

This is Method #18: Combination of various effects.

For example, let's take three different physical effects.

The first effect is the light polarization phenomenon. It is known that if light passes through some special substances, it will be polarized. The oscillations would be only in one plane — for example, in the vertical one.

The second effect is the effect of special crystals which change the angle of incidence as polarized light passes through the crystal.

The Third effect is the expansion of objects when heat is applied.

If you combine these three phenomena, you will get a thermometer. The higher the temperature, the thicker the plate, and therefore polarized light will pass through the plate at a bigger angle.

The laws of combination of these effects are not known as yet. But this is a frontier of inventive science that will lead to new solutions for many inventive problems.

Chapter 17
The Ribbon Invented by Moebius

In the story written by the science fiction author Arthur C. Clarke, "The Wall of Darkness," the sage Greil said to his companion Braildon, "Here is a flat sheet. It has, of course, two sides. Can you imagine this sheet with only one side?"

Braildon looked at him in surprise. "It is impossible," he said.

"Yes, at first glance, it is impossible," Greil said. "Take a strip of paper, it has two sides. It is possible to glue the ends of the strip to make a ring. The two sides will remain, an outside and an inside. What will happen if we twist one end of the strip 180⁰, and after that we glue the ends?"

Greil connected both ends of the twisted strip. "Now slide your finger over one side," quietly said Greil. Breildon decided not to do that. He understood what the old wise man had in mind.

"I understand!" he said. "There are no longer two separate planes. Now we have only one continuous plane, a one-sided plane."

This twisted ribbon received the name **Moebius ribbon**, after the name of the German mathematician who first described its wonderful properties.

This is Method #19: Geometrical effect of the Moebius ribbon.

Try to imagine an ant that is traveling on the outside surface of the Moebius ring. If the ant does not cross the edge of the ribbon, but travels along its surface, it will come back to the starting point. On the Moebius ribbon the traveling time of the ant will be twice as long then if it traveled over an ordinary ribbon ring. The ant will walk over both sides of the ring — outside and inside. This type of trip — on an unknown planet — was made by one of the heroes of the story "The Wall of Darkness." You may say that this was a fantasy, but today this wonderful characteristic of the Moebius ribbon is used by people to solve many different inventive problems.

Try to imagine a conventional belt formed into a ring. The outside surface of it is covered with an abrasive material. The belt is installed in a machine. When one needs to polish an object, one presses the object against the moving belt. After a while the abrasive surface wears out, and the belt must be replaced. This will create a lot of lost production time. What could we do to double the working time of the belt without increasing its length?

Several years ago a Russian inventor, A. Gubaidulin, got a patent for a sanding machine with a belt in the shape of the Moebius ribbon. The size of the belt was the same, but the working surface was doubled and so was the life of the belt. A very smart solution, wasn't it?

There are belt filters to clean liquids. After a while these filters get clogged with sediment and should be replaced. Probably you have already figured out what should be done. Yes, a filter with a Moebius ribbon is patented. There is a patent on a tape recorder using a Moebius ribbon. In different countries about 100 patents have been issued on devices and machines that utilize the principle of the Moebius ribbon. This means that inventions are made not only when one applies the formula, "**tricks plus physics**," but also "**tricks plus geometry**."

There are two disks cut out of cardboard. Place one disk on a table and hold the other one over the first one. Connect the edges of these disks with wooden dowels. You will get a meshed cylinder, similar to the wheel in a squirrel cage. Now turn the upper disk clockwise and the other disk counterclockwise. A curvilinear shape of the figure will appear, with a thin "waist," that looks like an hourglass. The greater the relative turning angle, the thinner the waist. This shape is called a rotating hyperboloid, and it has many characteristics that attract a lot of inventors' imaginations. The surface of the hyperboloid is curvilinear, although it was made of straight, linear parts. Therefore it is easy to make.

The Shookhov Tower of the Moscow Telecenter is a hyperboloid. The tower is made of linear metal members. The twisted shape brings great stability and strength. To build this kind of tower with other curvilinear forms would be very difficult. It would require curvilinear metal parts.

One of the most important characteristics of the hyperboloid is that it can change its shape very easily. Just turn one side or the other side, and the curvature is changed. This characteristic was used in many inventions. In Japan, for instance, hyperboloid rolls for a conveyor belt have been patented. The curvature of the hyperboloid rolls could be changed, and therefore the curvature of the conveyor belt as well. This is very important. During the transport of free flowing material, a curved belt is needed, and for the transport of boxes, a flat belt is needed.

This is Method #20: Geometrical effect of the Rotating Hyperboloid.

The following "formula" for an invention was published in Patent #426618: "A wheel for a potato-harvesting machine is comprised of two disks, connected with a number of thin rods. These rods have a flexible connection with the disks, and the disks are positioned on a shaft in such a way that one could turn over the other one."

The word "Hyperboloid" was not mentioned, although the characteristic of the hyperboloid was used to change the curvature.

There are many "geometrical inventions" based on the usage of paraboloids, spirals, etc. This means that inventors should know not only physics, but mathematics as well. However, inventors should not stop at mathematics. If we add the knowledge of chemistry, on the high school level, to our theory of problem solving, the inventor's arsenal would be much bigger and richer.

Chapter 18
Aim for the Ideal Final Result

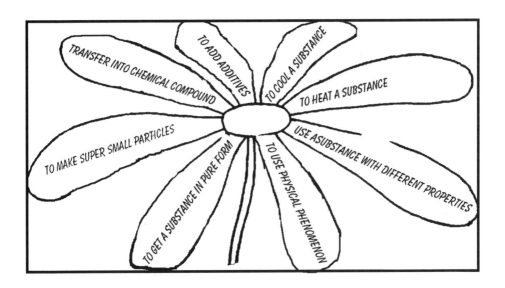

Recently the following event happened. An engineer was working on a process for a metal-plating lubricant. This is a conventional lubricant with an additive of two percent fine metallic powder. When a machine is working, the particles of metal settle on the rubbing surfaces and reduce wearing. The less clearance between the surfaces, the smaller the particles of powder should be in the lubricant. Here the technical contradiction appears: The smaller the particles, the better the lubricant — and the harder it is to make the lubricant.

To follow the theory for solving a technical problem, we should imagine the **Ideal Final Result (IFR)**. This means that we have to answer the following question: What would we want in an ideal solution? IFR is a fantasy, a dream. It cannot be reached, but it will allow us to build a path to the solution. Do you remember when we compared the theory of solving technical problems with a bridge? The IFR is one of the supports of that bridge.

What is the IFR in the lubricant problem? It is not difficult to answer. Ideally, the particles of metal should be reduced to their minimal limit — individual atoms. As you see, the theory provokes a paradoxical intimation: "Is it difficult to get very small particles of metal? Then it will be much easier to get super-small particles!"

At this point theory ends. To take the next step requires knowledge of chemistry.

Oil with suspended particles is a mechanical mixture. If we further break up particles we will get a colloidal solution. Finally, if we continue to break up the particles to the size of atoms we will get a real solution.

Now we can define IFR more accurately. The ideal final result is to have a solution of metal in oil — or more precisely, oil and with atoms of metal in it.

Unfortunately, this IFR cannot be reached. Even alchemists know that only one substance can be dissolved in a similar substance. Oil is an organic substance, and only another organic substance can be dissolved in it. Metal is not an organic substance. On the road to the Ideal Solution lies the following physical contradiction: The atoms of metal should be dissolved in the oil (this is our goal), but they cannot be dissolved (the laws of chemistry cannot be broken). Let us take one step back from IFR. Let us dissolve not atoms of metal, but molecules that include a metal. We will use a method already known to you: **Do a little less** than is required by IFR. If it is impossible to make particles as small as atoms, then we will make them a little bigger. We will make them molecules. The contradiction immediately disappears. There are no atoms of metal in the oil (there are molecules), and there are atoms of the metal in the oil (they are hidden in the molecules).

One problem is left to be solved: What kind of molecules should be used? There is only one necessary characteristic. The molecules should have a metal and should be organic. This means that it should be a metal-organic compound. It will dissolve in oil easily and will have a metal atom.

In order to solve this problem, we had to use several different concepts: IFR, Physical Contradiction, the Method "Do a Little Less," and a simple rule from chemistry — a substance can be dissolved only in similar substances. Even in this situation the problem was not yet solved. The molecules of a metal-organic substance have atoms of metal, although we need the atoms of metal to be separate. We have to recall the Laws of Chemistry again. In order to separate the atoms of metal from the molecules, the molecules need to be broken up. How can we do that? It is very simple: *We have to heat the substance to a certain temperature.* The oil will heat up when the machine is working. If we take a metalloorganic substance that breaks up at that temperature, the task is solved.

This is Method #21: Ideal Final Result (IFR).

Let us now see how this problem was solved in real life:

An engineer was looking for a solution using trial and error. He tried various methods of breaking up metal, made many experiments, and looked through the literature for a solution. Years passed. Once, he was in a book store and heard somebody asking for a handbook on metalloorganic compounds.

The engineer thought, "First, metalloorganic substances include metal, and second, they are organic substances. This means that such compounds can be dissolved in oil. This is what we are looking for!"

The engineer bought the book, found the proper information, and picked up the proper substance — cadmium salt of acetic acid.

In stories about inventions very often similar incidents are described. They are typical methods of Trial and Error. The person looks for a solution at random, and does not realize that the task could have been solved by using a scientific method: Formulate the **IFR** and determine the physical contradiction.

The task in the beginning seems tough, and the person tries everything they see or hear: It happened that somebody came into the bookstore and asked for a book on metalloorganic substances. If that had not happened, nobody knows how long this problem would have remained unsolved, and for how many years the engineer would have looked for the solution.

In one of the previous chapters, we formulated the following method:

"If it is necessary to introduce another substance into an existing one, and for some reason it is prohibited, then a slightly changed existing substance could be used as an agent."

What does that mean — "slightly changed" — in our problem?

The changes might be **physical** — heat it up, cool it down, use the same substance in different physical states, and so on. The changes might be **chemical**: use a substance not in its pure condition but in a compound form out of which the agent can be extracted. Or, take a simple substance and transfer it into a chemical compound after it has done its work.

This is Method #22: Introduction of a second substance.

I will give you one more example of how to use this method.

Crystals of aluminum oxide grow only from a very pure melt. It is forbidden to grow aluminum oxide crystals even in a platinum crucible because the atoms of platinum could get into the melt. In reality, this is an inventive problem with a purely physical contradiction. We must have a crucible to make a melt and we cannot have a crucible in order to have a pure melt. This means we must melt the aluminum oxide in... aluminum oxide. We will take any container, fill it up with aluminum oxide, and heat it in such a way that only the central part will melt. Now we have a melt of aluminum oxide in a crucible of solid aluminum oxide. To achieve that we will use electromagnetic induction. The source of energy in our case will not have any contact with the heated substance.

Everything is fine at this moment, except that aluminum oxide is a dielectric, and does not conduct electric current. This means that there is no electromagnetic induction. Although the melted aluminum oxide can conduct current, in order to get a melt the aluminum oxide has to be heated. But we cannot heat the aluminum oxide because it is a dielectric.

This happens very often — solve one contradiction, another will appear, and then a third. It's like an obstacle race — one barrier after another.

Here is the physical contradiction: Pieces of metal must be added into the aluminum oxide in order to create electromagnetic induction, and it is forbidden to add it into the aluminum oxide in order to keep this substance pure. The invention that helped overcome this contradiction was surprisingly simple. Pieces of aluminum were added to the aluminum oxide before the fusion. Aluminum is a very good conductor of electricity. During the electromagnetic induction, it will generate heat and will melt together with the aluminum oxide. After a while at a high temperature, the aluminum will be burned, turning into aluminum oxide, and will not pollute the oxide.

72

Try now to solve a simple problem. In order to get the answer you have to follow only two steps.

Step one: Imagine the Ideal Final Result. Act as if you are a magician and objects obey your commands.

Step two: Think of how to get the Ideal Result without reconstruction and with the least changes.

Problem 33
The tank reported politely

Today many people use propane gas for their household needs. The gas is usually stored in metal tanks. When a little fuel is left in the tank, the owner should think about refilling it. The question is: How to determine the amount of gas left in the tank?

Engineers from a large gas company have been trying to solve this kind of problem. The method should be simple, easy to use, and allow to determine when the last ten percent of the propane gas is in the tank.

"Measure the pressure of the propane?" pondered one of the engineers. "No, that is no good. As long as one drop of propane is left in the tank the pressure will be the same, because the used-up gas will be replenished from the liquid propane by means of evaporation."

"What if we weigh it?" asked another engineer. "No, this is no good either. It is very difficult to disconnect and reconnect the tank for that purpose every time you want to know the amount that is left."

And suddenly the inventor appeared.

"I know the ideal solution," he said. "The tank should report about the balance by itself very politely." And he explained how to reach that ideal solution.

What can you offer? Keep in mind that the use of glass tubing is prohibited, because it is dangerous.

Chapter 19
Order in the "Brain's Attic"

Now is the time for the reader to be resentful. This book started with a criticism of the "Trial and Error" method where, in order to solve a complicated problem, one has to randomly pick out many variants. It takes years, and there is no guarantee that one will find the right solution.

A theory was developed: Laws, Rules, Formula. Take the formula, and without too much effort, solve the problem. Very good! Suddenly it was found that we have to know the Law of Technical Evolution, many methods and tricks like "the substance *exists* and it *does not exist*," the Laws of S-Field analysis, etc.

Further, we have to know physics, the inventive characteristics of physical effects, and other phenomena. We also have to know mathematics and chemistry. We are sure that we will have to learn biology later. In nature there are a lot of hidden patents.

Maybe it is easier to continue inventing as we did 5000 years ago? Yes, it is simpler to invent in the old ways. It is easier to dig a pit with a shovel, than to run an excavator. Walking is much easier than driving a car. For speed, power, and effectiveness of any action one should pay the price by using knowledge. Inventiveness is no longer an exception. If you want to solve a complicated problem, learn the theory, conquer "inventive physics" and the whole of science.

By the way, we are at a very interesting point here. To solve an inventive problem it is not as important to have so much knowledge as it is to organize the knowledge that one already has.

Today a student in school knows a lot, but that information is not organized. The effectiveness with which he can use this knowledge is very low — as low as one or two percent. I am talking about school, because that is when we learn a lot and remember a lot, but we do not learn to use it in practice. Our knowledge is organized like a bad warehouse — in bulk without sorting.

Do you remember the problem about the weevils? After this problem was published in the *Pioneer's Truth* magazine there were many letters, and more than half had the following answer: "Take a cup, place 200 weevils in it, measure the temperature with a regular thermometer, and then divide the result by the number of weevils."

This was written by students from the fifth and eighth grades! If one would ask them:

"What is the temperature of your fist if the temperature of each finger is 36^0 C? Nobody will say 180^0. Life's experience contradicts this. In the process of solving a problem similar to that of the weevils, this type of mistake is made frequently. Knowledge about heat energy and temperature is not sufficiently understood, and it lies like a dead weight in the warehouse of our memory.

How can we revive this knowledge?

If we can trust Sir Arthur Conan Doyle, one of the first to stumble over that problem was Sherlock Holmes. Before Holmes, criminal problems were solved by the method of "Trial and Error." Holmes developed a system, and of course found it necessary to have a big reserve of active knowledge. The following was said by Holmes:

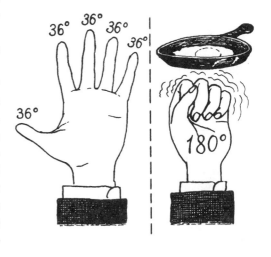

"I consider that a man's brain originally is like a little empty attic, and you have to stock it with such furniture as you choose. A fool takes in all the lumber of every sort that he comes across, so that the knowledge which might be useful to him gets crowded out, or at best is jumbled up with a lot of other things, so that he has a difficulty in laying his hands upon it. Now, the skillful workman is very careful indeed as to what he takes into his brain-attic. He will have nothing but the tools which may help him in doing his work, but of these he has a large assortment, and all in the most perfect order."

The selection of knowledge made by a school program is done well in theory. Each page of a textbook on physics, chemistry, mathematics, and biology might be the strongest tool in the problem solving process. The idea is to bring life into knowledge, understand it, and to get a sense of its creative power. When you solve a technical problem with the use of physical phenomena, it is as though you are learning about it for the first time, and discovering something new and interesting.

This could be related even to knowledge beyond the boundaries of a school program. These facts could also be used as tools for creativity — yet this knowledge is dumped into the brain's attic absolutely without any order.

Let us now look into a very interesting task. Kindergarten knowledge is enough to solve this problem, if this knowledge is stored in an orderly fashion.

Problem 34
Where the wind blows from

On one of the farms, new cow barns were built. The air in the barns had to be clean, and the owner of the farm invited some scientists to determine if the ventilation was sufficient.

"We have to study the air movement in the barns," said one of the scientists. "We will measure the velocity of the air streams. The barns are big, and the ceilings are high. The air velocity depends on the temperature of the walls and the roof. It will take a lot of measurements, and a couple of months of work."

And suddenly the inventor appeared.

"While you were having a meeting, I got the measurements from the first barn," he said. "Measurements were made from every point, even under the roof. This is so simple...."

How did the inventor get his result? Let us try not to guess.

We start from the IFR. The Ideal Solution is: "In any place in the barn, by our wish, arrows appear, showing the direction and velocity of the air." How do we achieve this? Suppose we take a lighted candle, and watch the position of the flame. It is okay if we have to make measurements in ten — or even a hundred — places. The IFR said: "In any place!" Therefore the candle is not effective enough. The flame is "tied" to the candle. It is impossible to fill the barn with flames. Maybe we can fill the barn with smoke? This is no good either. The smoke would be everywhere, but smoke is not transparent, and we will not be able to see and to measure anything. To achieve IFR it takes something that has contradictory characteristics: It should be everywhere, in every place, and it should not be everywhere in order to keep the air clear, so that we can see through it.

It is a very familiar situation. It requires us to add something to the air, and it prohibits us from adding something to the air. The flame and the smoke are no good, because they meet only the first half of the requirement. We are going to do exactly as we did in the previous tasks. We will add bits of other air to the barn air with only a small change to make it visible.

How to color a bit of air? There are only two methods of adding color to air. We can color the whole piece or its surface — air surrounded by a thin film.

Probably you have already found the solution. We are talking about soap bubbles. Many soap bubbles will make the air visible in the barn. In places with a higher velocity of air, the photo will show long lines of bubbles.

I am sure that the knowledge about soap bubbles and their properties was in our brain's attic for a long time, but it was lying there like a "dead" weight. Now you know that soap bubbles and suds (a system that is made out of many bubbles) satisfy very well the contradictory characteristic: **There is a substance and there is no substance.**

This is Method #23: Utilization of soap bubbles and foam.

This means that the use of soap bubbles in different problems, as a solution, is a very strong method. The previous problem allows us to get the feeling of the "beauty" of that method.

We have dusted off our new tool, and placed it with others in the proper order.

Chapter 20
Being an Inventor is a Profession of the Future

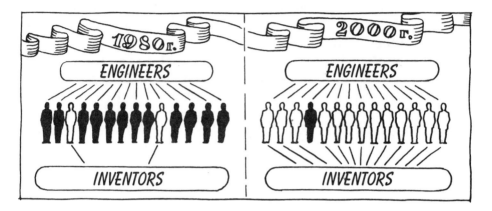

The profession of "Inventor" does not exist at this time. An engineer performing his duty incidentally could invent. You can argue: "What about Edison? He received more than a thousand patents!" Edison was working on his inventions mainly by using the method of Trial and Error. To develop a new battery, he did 50,000+ experiments. This is not possible for one person, and Edison was not working alone. There were about a thousand people working for him in the laboratory. His laboratory can be considered an Inventive Firm. It was exactly that — a firm, not just one person.

We say Morse was the inventor of the telegraph. Popov was the inventor of the radio. Fulton was the inventor of the steamboat. Not one of them was a professional inventor. They worked on one or several inventive problems, and then they were too busy to introduce the product to the market. James Watt was a professional mechanic. He invented the steam engine, patented his invention, solved a couple of other problems, and to the end of his life was a professional businessman who thought about getting profits out of his inventions.

The inventor who was trying to live by solving inventive problems usually died in poverty. This is not a surprise. The method of Trial and Error will not guarantee that the task will be solved in a short time. The painter knows the time he needs to finish his painting. The writer knows how many years he needs to write a novel. The inventor who uses the method of Trial and Error cannot say how soon he will solve a problem. Maybe the solution will come today, or maybe a lifetime will not be enough.

Can you imagine an inventive department with professionals, who are solving different inventive problems by the "Trial and Error" method? People are sitting and thinking, randomly picking up one variant after another.

"My friend," the Head of the department would say. "You have been thinking for ten years, but with no result."

"It is a very difficult problem," the inventor would say. "I have looked through six thousand possible solutions."

"I suggest you should take a walk on the street," the boss would say. "Maybe you will find something that will prompt you to the solution."

"I prefer to take a nap," the professional would answer. "A new idea sometimes appears in a dream. You know similar cases...."

This is no exaggeration. Recently in *Psychology* magazine an article was published about an American psychologist, McKinnon, who was trying to find the source of enlightenment and intuition by studying the transition period between deep sleep and awakening. A similar study has been going on for about sixty or seventy years. There is still no result.

The method of "Trial and Error" has exhausted its possibilities. Therefore, efforts to improve this method bring no result.

A different method is required to produce inventions — a method based on the use of laws of evolution of technical systems.

During the past several years special groups have appeared to solve problems by implementing the **Theory of Solving Inventive Problem (TRIZ)**. Soon these groups will become common, in the same way as it happened with the profession of "Computer Programmer." Probably, the experts in TRIZ will be called Engineer-Inventor, or Technical Systems Development Engineer.

Let us fantasize a little bit. We will try to look into a room of one of these inventive organizations that does not exist yet.

Problem 35
Invention by request

A factory produced a microthin wire. Push a button and a very high-speed machine starts to make a thin, silver web-like wire which then winds onto a big reel. The machine is good, but the control of the diameter of the wire was very primitive. The machine was usually stopped, a piece of wire was cut off and weighed. By knowing the specific gravity of the wire, the diameter of the wire was calculated. Many methods were tried to measure the diameter during the process. Nothing came out of it, either the method was too complicated or not accurate enough.

One day the supervisor of the shop went to a concert. When the guitar player came out on the stage, the supervisor suddenly felt stunned.

"Eureka!" he said.

The next day the engineer told his associates about his idea. The wire looks like a guitar string. The frequency of the string depends on its diameter. We have to vibrate the micro-wire, and the frequency of the vibration will tell us about the diameter. The invention was adapted in two days, and the machine now worked without stopping.

"Very good," said the boss, signing the paper for the inventor's bonus. "Now, starting with the new year, we are going to produce an even thinner wire. The diameter should be measured with very high accuracy. We need another method. What should we do? Wait two more years until somebody will have another flash of an idea? Let's make a request and seek a solution to the problem from the experts."

The next day the engineer went to the inventors' group.

"This is a very simple problem," said the manager of the inventors' group. "Let's go to the next room, there is a new trainee over there, he will help you."

The trainee was very young. The engineer stated the problem to the trainee with great skepticism.

"This problem can be solved very easily," said the trainee. "First we should write down the conditions. There is a substance S_1, the wire. This substance should produce a signal, a Field F, that will carry the information about the diameter of the wire."

On a piece of paper he drew:

"The substance by itself cannot produce this type of field," he continued. "That means that we should apply another field."

"This is an S-Field diagram of the invention, made at your factory," explained the trainee. "To strike the string means to apply a mechanical field F_m that produces the mechanical vibrations. Those vibrations are mechanical field F_2.

To increase the accuracy of the measurements, **first**, we should replace the mechanical fields with an electromagnetic one; **second**, we should finish building the S-Field by introducing a second substance S_2.

The new diagram will look like this:

The electromagnetic field F_1 affects the wire S_1. The wire will interact with the second substance, S_2, that will send the signal — some form of field F_2 — that carries the information about the diameter of the wire. What kind of signal do you prefer?"

"A light signal," the engineer said. "It is more convenient."

"This means that F_2 is an optical field. Thus, the electromagnetic field F_{EL} affects the wire S_1. The wire affects some substance S_2, and that substance sends a light signal F_2 about the diameter of the wire. The problem is solved. What we have to do now is to recall the physics of the tenth grade. Please look...."

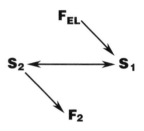

He handed the engineer an open textbook.

"You are probably right," the engineer said thoughtfully after he had read the page in the book. "It is a very good solution! Strange that we could not guess it ourselves!"

We have to measure the diameter of the micro-wire. The "Corona Discharge" could appear very easily on the thin wires. The discharge depends on the diameter of the wire. It is exactly what we need to solve the problem! The brightness and the shape of the "Crown" will signal us about the diameter of the wire, and the shape of its cross-section. If the cross-section is an oval the "Corona discharge" is also an oval.

The next story is a real one. In one of the Schools of Technical Science (where this method is taught), there was a student-mathematician. He graduated from the University and got a job in another town. Very soon he wrote a letter, where he described this very interesting problem.

Problem 36
An accuracy within one degree

In the hall of a scientific company the director stopped a new young mathematician.

"As I remember, you graduated from one of the Inventors` School?" he said. "Frankly, my opinion is that everything depends on the natural talent of the individual, but.... We are going to form another group. There is a big project ahead, and the problem is very complicated. We do not even know how to start. The group consists of fifteen people. I was thinking of bringing you into that group."

The mathematician was curious. He asked, "What kind of problem is it?"

The director explained: "Pest grubs sometimes get into the food grain. Naturally, they should be destroyed before the grain is packaged. The best solution is to heat the grain to 65° C, no higher, and no lower, otherwise everything is going to be damaged. It is ideal to control the heating process within one degree of accuracy.

"However, the heating of big volumes of grain created overheating in some areas. If the process is done with small amounts of grain, production drops tremendously. We tried many ways of heating the grain, but nothing worked. We would like to try one more method — blow heated air through the layers of grain. Maybe we will be lucky enough to find a working solution."

"You do not need to do that," the mathematician interrupted. "The problem should be solved like this...."

And he explained the solution.

Probably you have already found the solution. Ferromagnetic powder with a Curie point of 65° C should be added to the grain. When electromagnetic induction is applied, the grain would be heated exactly to 65° C. After the grain is processed the magnetic powder is removed with a magnetic filter.

The letter from the mathematician ended like this, "My interlocutor looked at me for several minutes, completely shocked. I never thought that the solution to the problem could bring such a reaction. People were walking along the hall saying "Hi!" to the boss, but he did not reply, and continued looking at me...."

82

Chapter 21
A Little Bit of Practice

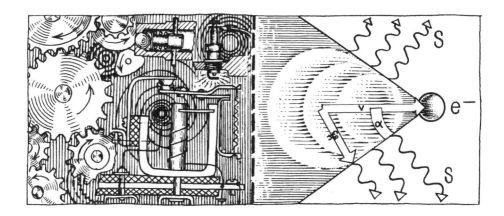

Now we can add some more methods on our list.

(12) S-Field Analysis.
(13) Self-Service.
(14) Heat expansion.
(15) Transition from macrostructure to microstructure.
(16) Corona discharge.
(17) Curie point of ferromagnetic materials.
(18) Combination of various effects.
(19) Geometrical effect of Moebius Ribbon.
(20) Geometrical effect of Rotating Hyperboloid.
(21) Ideal Final Result (IFR).
(22) Introduction of a second substance.
(23) Utilization of soap bubbles and foam.

You already know the first thing you need to do — once the problem is stated — is formulate the **Ideal Final Result** (**IFR**) and try to achieve it. A good solution is always close to the IFR. Let's practice with this "tool."

Problem 37
Let's throw the screw out

Someone looking into a microscope needs to move the glass plate, and the object on it, sometimes only a hundredth or a thousandth of a millimeter — almost the size of a hair. To do this, one usually uses a screw type mechanism to move the slide holding this glass. It is a very complicated and expensive process to manufacture such parts.

The engineers got together and asked: "What can we do to make the mechanism more accurate, more reliable and cost less?"

They started to think.

"There is a technical contradiction," said one engineer. "Screws with high accuracy are very expensive and wear out fast. And a coarser thread will not have the required accuracy."

And suddenly the inventor appeared.

"Let's dump the screw!" he said. "What means should we use to achieve higher accuracy in the movement of a glass slide?"

You will solve **Problem #37** for sure, even without reading the problem to the end. If you have read this chapter carefully, you can offer three correct answers.

Problem 38
Something simpler

All polymers get old. This process reminds us of the oxidation of metal, because oxygen is the "guilty party." It breaks down the molecules of polymers. To protect polymers from oxygen it is necessary to add a fine iron powder to the "boiling" polymer. The atoms of iron will take in the oxygen and protect the polymer. However, the finer the powder, the faster it will interact with oxygen — even before the powder is added into the polymer. The resulting iron oxide will lose its protective characteristics.

"We have to use an inert gas as the environment for that purpose," said the chemist, who was invited as a consultant.

"It is going to be very complicated and inconvenient," objected the engineers from the factory. "We need something simpler."

And here the Inventor appeared.

"Please!" he said. "There is a very simple solution."

What do you think the Inventor offered? You will find the solution very easy. Try to think of an idea that is practical.

Problem 39
Powder on the conveyor

A conveyor line from one building to another was installed in a mine. A very fine ore is transported from one conveyor to another until it reaches the kilns. Workers complained to the engineer that the ore was like powder, and blew off the conveyor with just a light breeze.

"What can we do?" said the engineer. "We are watering that powder with no result, because the water evaporates very fast. Too much water is no good either. Maybe we have to cover the conveyor? Then you will have more work to do: to open and close the conveyor...."

And suddenly the inventor appeared.

"We should have a cover in order to prevent the ore from blowing away," he said. "And we should not have a cover in order to simplify the work. Therefore, it should be...."

What do you think should be done? Keep in mind that we have to retain the conveyor. The task is to prevent dust development.

Part 4
The Art of Inventing

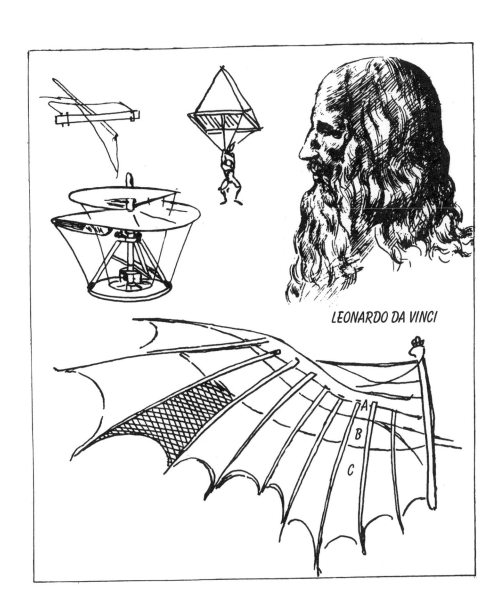

LEONARDO DA VINCI

Chapter 22
The Roads We Choose

Inventive activity has many sides. It involves finding the problem, solving it, turning a new idea into a working model and bringing the device or method to life. Of course the most important thing is to find the solution. Some of the stages of that process could be turned over to professionals in that area, like transferring the idea into a model, and then developing the model into the final product. Of course it is better if the inventor himself takes part in all these stages. However, it is necessary and sufficient for the author to take part only in the problem solving process, where nobody can replace the inventor. The solution to the problem is the essence of invention.

Inventors of the 19th century were "Jacks of all trades." They built new machines with their hands, and improved them until they worked properly. The contemporary inventor is first of all a thinker — an intellectual. It is very good if the inventor is a handyman. Still, the most important attribute that the inventor needs is to have a very precise intellectual process of thinking. Before one starts to draw-up anything, one should develop an idea of the solution, and this is a very complicated process.

In the beginning, the inventor should ask the question: "Should I tackle this task, or reject it and replace it with another task that will achieve the original goal?"

In reality, the question is whether the old system has used up all its resources or not. If the reserves are gone, then it is time to develop a new system. Let us take a look at how this question appears, and how we should answer it, by using a specific example.

Problem 40
Stop guessing

During the melting process of ore in blast furnaces, clinker is produced — a mixture of magnesium and calcium oxide. Clinker at a temperature of about 1000^0 C is dumped into big buckets and delivered by railroad to plants for reprocessing. Melted clinker is a very good raw material to manufacture construction materials. Although cooled clinker is no longer a good raw material, it is not economical to melt it again. At the beginning the clinker in the bucket is liquid. However, during transportation a crust develops. It takes a special large mechanism to break the crust. The crust, even with a man-made hole, will keep some of the liquid clinker inside the bucket. As a result, only 2/3 of the liquid clinker is used at the reprocessing plant. The rest of it is dumped out as junk. Meanwhile, it takes a lot of labor to clean the bucket of hardened clinker, and to remove the waste from the plant's grounds.

Finally, a Scientific Committee was formed to solve this problem.

"A bucket with very good insulation should be designed," offered one of the scientists.

"We tried that — it does not work," objected one member of the plant team. "Insulation takes a lot of space, the bucket will be very wide and that is not acceptable, according to railroad regulations."

"What about a lid for the bucket?" the scientists continued. "Why can't we make the lid with heavy insulation? The main portion of the heat loss goes through the top, where the hot clinker has contact with the air."

"We tried that as well," sighed the plant member. "The bucket is the size of a room. Can you imagine a lid of that size? That lid would have to be put on and taken off by a crane! Too much work!"

"I think we have to tackle the problem differently," said a second scientist. "Let us think about reconstructing the whole process in such a way that we do not need to move the clinker so far away."

"I am not sure, I am not sure," objected another scientist. "I would offer to state the problem a little bit differently: Let's find a faster way to deliver the clinker."

"We all have to look at the root of the problem," said the fourth scientist. The task should be much wider — to produce iron without getting clinker as a by-product."

And suddenly the inventor appeared.

"Stop guessing," he said. "The problem should be formulated so that...."

How do you think the problem should be formulated? .

In reality, we have a pile of tasks — so-called inventive situations — and it is really difficult to choose the right one, the one that will produce the best result.

Problem 41
Let us discuss the situation

In order to manufacture a sheet of glass, a ribbon of glass is heated to a red color and is fed onto a conveyor. The ribbon moves from one supporting roll to another and it slowly cools off.

After that, the glass has to be polished for some time because the ribbon, still being hot and flexible, sags while going from roll to roll, and the surface becomes uneven. Engineers, who faced this problem for the first time, offered to make the diameter of the rolls as small as possible. The smaller the rolls, the less sagging of the glass will occur. This means that the glass can come out more uniform.

A technical contradiction appears here. The smaller the rolls, the more difficult it is to manufacture a conveyor of several meters long. Let's say that the diameter of each roll is equal to the size of a match, then every meter of the conveyor will have 500 rolls, and their installation will require the accuracy of a jeweler. What if the rolls had the diameter of a thread?

"There's nothing to fear," said one young engineer. "There are crafty people around, who can make a drawing even on a poppy seed. Let's design a conveyor with very thin rolls. We can find people to assemble this type of conveyor."

"Listen, think about the cost of that conveyor," someone contradicted the young fellow. "It is better to have big rolls. What we have to do is to improve the process of polishing the glass. We have to straighten out the ribs on the glass."

"I think that we have to throw the conveyor out of the line," offered somebody else. "It would be good to replace it with something radically new."

And suddenly the inventor appeared.

"Let's look into this situation," he said. "Out of all those tasks we should choose...."

And he explained what task he would prefer. What do you think?

It is very easy to tackle Problems #40 and #41.

In **Problem #40** there is a system called "Transportation of clinker." This system is part of the higher system "Iron Production."

We have no problem with the higher system, we do not need to change it. The system does its own work: transports clinker. Everything is fine except that part of the clinker gets hard during transportation. It does not make sense to change the whole system — and of course, not the higher system. It is foolish to refuse to have a car just because the windshield gets dirty.

In such situations transition to the problem is made by using a very simple rule: "Everything is left as it is, except that the shortcomings should disappear." Let's transport the clinker as we did before, in open buckets without hard crust developing.

In **Problem #41** the picture is different. The system could not perform its basic duty. **First**, the conveyor should form a straight glass ribbon. **Second**, the conveyor should move the ribbon out of the kiln. We have exhausted the possibilities for further development of the rollers (not in general, but in the process of glass production), and it needs to be replaced by a new system.

Perhaps, other cases are possible among these two mentioned. If you are not really sure which way to go — whether to save the existing system or look for a new one — then you have to formulate the problem in such a way as to save the original system.

No exact science can exclude skill. For example, different results can be obtained by different people using the same telescope. The results depend on the skill of the user and the goal.

Suppose that the task is to replace a conventional ship with something completely new. The ship is a "System" that works on a macrolevel. The body, the prop, the engine are very big parts. One day this system will be transferred to the microlevel, although it is difficult to imagine how this ship will look at the microlevel. What can the theory of solving inventive problems say about this?

First, the transition to the microlevel is possible in general terms.

Second, the system "Ship" has not entered into the third stage of its development when a rigid, solid structure is transformed into a flexible and moveable one. The resources for the development of the system are not exhausted yet. This means that many decades may pass before the transition to the microlevel takes place. That's it!

Here the theory is ended. Choosing the task is up to the individual. The individual has to make a decision as to which direction to take. One has to have a clear picture. If one chooses to develop a completely new technical system when the old one is not exhausted in its development, the road to success and acceptance by society is very harsh and long. A task that is far ahead of its time is not easy to solve. And the most difficult task is to prove that a new system is possible and necessary. In the previous chapter I mentioned the vibrogyroscope. The author applied for a patent in 1954 — and got it in 1975, twenty-one years later. It took two decades to prove its usefulness and its possibility of construction.

Imagine that two hundred years ago an inventor came to the ship builders and said: "Why do you bother with sails? Throw them away and install a steam engine that people use now in mines. Let the engine turn the paddle wheel like a water mill. That will be great!"

I doubt that anybody would have taken this seriously — that we were talking about one of the great inventions, the *Steamboat*.

A.G. Presniakov from the USSR applied for his patent in 1955, and got a rejection. All the experts revolted. It was considered absurd to throw out engines and replace them with electromagnetic pumps! The inventor spent fourteen years arguing and proving his position. Only in 1969 did he get his patent. It took him fourteen years to be recognized by scientific and technical experts.

But there were many other steps to be taken before his invention would see the world — designs, models, experiments, and so on....

Boats with the Presniakov engine do not exist yet, although, with time, they will appear.

The transition of technical systems into microlevel is a law. But the Law of Evolution in the development of technical systems states: **the system should exhaust its resources before it moves to the microlevel.**

Alexander Presniakov has not received his reward for his invention yet. His boat is still only on paper. But credit for being the first person to invent a boat with a magnetohydrodynamic engine will belong to A. Presniakov. The joy and satisfaction of creativity, the thought that you have solved a task of the future — this is a real reward for an inventor. Society is a winner as well. When the time comes to change the system "Ship" into a microlevel, one of the directions will be known to scientists. Inventions that were made ahead of their time, in the final analysis, are very substantial and practical.

There is another road. The system "Ship" has not aged yet. One can direct efforts and energy toward solving relatively small problems on macrolevels by improving different parts of the ship. In several years one can get many patents for improvements, introduce them to the market, reap benefits, and hear words of gratitude from people whose work you have helped to ease.

Problem 42
Rain is not a hindrance

A ship was being loaded at a dock. A very powerful crane lowered skids with sacks through an opening down on the deck. There was a heavy rain, and water was coming into the storage compartment.

"What kind of weather is this?" rumbled one loader inside the ship. "I am completely soaked."

"There is nothing you can do about it," answered another. "During loading time you cannot close the hatch or put a roof over it."

And suddenly the Inventor appeared.

"You need a very special roof," he said. "A roof that will stop the rain and allow the cargo to go through. Take a look...."

What kind of roof did he offer?

Thousands of ships are anchored at docks. Tens of thousands of workers are working under the sun, snow or rain. A roof over the storage compartment is definitely needed. It is not so difficult to invent one. A similar problem appeared a long time ago. To prevent a draft in a factory, doors should be closed. To allow a forklift to go through the door, it should

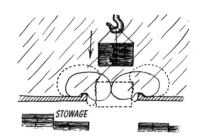

be open. The contradiction was eliminated very easily — the door was made out of heavy, flexible, transparent strips. The forklift could get through when it needed to, and the door was closed all the time. The size of the compartment hatch is much larger than a regular door, therefore a roof door could be made out of air sacks and placed over the hatch like a two-sided roof. The cargo could push those sacks aside, get through the hatch down to the compartment. A patent on this idea was issued very quickly.

It is necessary to solve different problems: small, middle sized, large and very large. The shortcomings of the "Trial and Error" method becomes more obvious as the size of the problem increases.

Therefore, big companies work on the improvements of existing large systems and very seldom on the development of completely new ones.

With this new theory of solving technical problems the whole situation is changing. We are confident that in the near future innovation institutions will be organized whose main specialty will be the search for solutions to tasks of the distant future.

The most advantageous situation is when a system exhausts its growth and needs to be replaced today with a new one based on other principles. The disadvantages of the old system are known to everyone, and new ideas are welcome. This is similar to Problem # 41. It is not beneficial to build thinner rolls. The conveyor with rolls should be replaced with something completely different in principle.

Chapter 23
Strange Mirrors of the Operator STC
(Size, Time, Cost)

Once people asked the Hodja Nasredin to make a miracle. "Okay," he said, "I will make a miracle on one condition. From now on none of you will think about a white monkey." Nasredin then described that monkey in great detail, and repeated: "Now, don't think about this monkey anymore."

Naturally, on the contrary, nobody could stop thinking about the white monkey.

The inventive problem, like wily Nasredin, imposes on you a "white monkey." In **Problem #41** we decided, without wavering, to get rid of the roller conveyor. However, the shape of the rollers or belt conveyor constantly appears before our internal vision. To let go of an habitual image is very difficult because we do not know how a new conveyor should look.

I remember one very interesting story. A factory produced millions of pieces of glazed pottery - cups and plates. Every piece was baked twice in a kiln. All wares were screened with respect to quality after the first baking stage. During the second baking stage special temperature conditions were set for dif-

94

ferent screening groups. The screening process was done with sound. The worker took a plate, hit it very gently with a special hammer, and then determined the degree of baking by the tone of the sound. Workers called this process "ringing the bell." This was not easy work. All the shift workers were banging plates or cups, listening to the sound and screening the product. Finally, some inventors decided to develop a robot for this task.

This was a typical case where the system had become obsolete and had to be replaced with something really new.

The inventors understood that, but they could not walk away from that "white monkey" image. A machine with two "hands" was built. The first hand held the plate while the second hand hit the plate with a hammer. A microphone picked up the sound and an electronic device analyzed it and commanded the first hand where to place the plate.

The machine was installed at the factory. And very soon it was found that the machine worked more slowly than the people. The inventors tried to increase the speed of the arms, but the machine started to break the plates. The machine was taken away and the workers continued to screen the product as they had done before.

At first glance the task was simple — replace human hands with mechanical ones. The human arm, palm, and fingers are tools that have the highest sensitivity and flexibility with the finest adjustments and control. The arm is controlled by the brain. This is a "Brain-Arm" system that took a million years to perfect.

In technical museums there are sewing machines, brick stackers, fruit pickers and so on, all with arms. All of them are not good because they are trying to imitate the human arm. In order to mechanize the work that the human arm and fingers are doing, one should find another way. Change the principle of action and find a new method — one that is easy to mechanize and to automate.

The Theory of Solving Inventive Problems offers a very special tool for your imagination: **This is Method #24: Operator STC (Size, Time, Cost).**

These are the questions that the inventor should consider:
What will happen if the **size** of an object is decreased?
Or, on the contrary, increased? What will happen if the **time**
for an action to take place decreases? Or, increases? What will
happen if new requirements are added — the **cost** of a machine
equals zero? Or, on the contrary, the cost is unlimited?

How is the problem going to be solved under these conditions? These three questions of Operator STC, like crooked mirrors in a "laughing room," distort the conditions of the task, and force our imagination to work and help get rid of the obtrusive image of the old system.

Can you imagine a plate the size of a dime, then an even smaller one, like a piece of dust? You cannot pick up such a plate with your fingers, or strike it with a hammer. For a plate like that a weightless hammer is needed. What if we increase the speed of the machine?

Let's say, that the plate is of normal size, but we have only 1 second for the test — 1/1000 of a second, 1/1,000,000 of a second? During that short period of time sound cannot get to the ears of the operator of the microphone. This means that something faster than sound is needed. Only light is faster than sound. What if the plates were struck by light? This is the weightless hammer! Could we catch the reflected light, and "listen" to it?

Operator STC is not supposed to give you the answer to your problem. It's task is only to break up our psychological inertia, which blocks our thinking process. The strange mirrors of Operator STC are only tools for the first step to work on solving problems.

If you have had experience with soldering, you know that the first step is to clean the surface with acids. A similar thing happens in our problem (and in our mind) when we use Operator STC. It happens many times, that after using that Operator, the problem becomes clear and easy to solve.

Take for example the problem of the glazed pottery. Operator STC prompted: it is good to replace the conventional hammer with a light. For screening plates, this is a new method. Maybe this method has already been used in other applications? Maybe people have already developed instruments for this test? Then we can take that device and adapt it for our test.

Where is it required to test ceramic parts? In the production of electric resistors. Everybody knows that. Of course those resistors have to be tested. In size they are much smaller than plates. Resistors cannot be tested with sound, so people use light for that purpose. The amount of light reflected from resistors depends on the degree of baking. The machine sorts thousands of resistors per hour. A small change in this device will make it possible to use it for testing plates, and will release the laborers from monotonous hard work.

Look at the *Official Gazette* magazine and you will see that we are on the right track. Small objects are tested not with sound, but with light. For instance, a grain of rice, that is "cooked" by the sun could be controlled by light. There is a patent on that process.

Look at what is happening! By utilizing Operator STC we are deliberately complicating the problem, and at the same time we are searching for a simplified solution! This is happening because Operator STC helps us get rid of our psychological inertia, and enables us to look at the problem without prejudice.

Problem 43
Investigation is done by experts

"This rifle should be examined," said an investigator as he placed the rifle on the table before the expert. "I have to know whether or not this rifle fired a bullet a week ago."

The expert looked carefully at the rifle and nodded his head, "I don't know how to tackle this task. The barrel has been cleaned and there are no carbon deposits."

And suddenly the inventor appeared.

"I know how to examine it," he said. "Let us use Operator STC."

Suppose that shot was fired a day ago, one hour ago, five minutes ago. By the specifications of the task there is no carbon deposit inside the barrel. If the shot was made ten seconds ago, then the barrel should be warm. Then we could say even with closed eyes whether or not the shot was fired. Because the temperature memory is very short, we cannot rely on it after a short while.

Let us find some other "memory" that metal may have. What properties change during the firing of a rifle? Do you remember **Problem #32** about heating the high voltage power lines? Steel is demagnetized when the temperature is above the Curie point. It's magnetic characteristics disappear from shock as well. The gas from gunpowder hits not only the bullet, but the inside surface of the barrel as well. Usually the barrel has some magnetic properties, because of the magnetic field of the Earth. After the shot is fired the barrel is demagnetized. During the next three to four weeks the barrel regains its magnetic characteristics. The more time passes, the closer to normal the magnetic properties of the rifle will be. It is enough to compare the magnetic properties of two rifles in order to determine which rifle was used a week ago.

In our case, Operator STC helped to uncover only half of the path to the answer. It reminded us about "temperature memory." In order to switch to the "magnetic memory" one should recall some physics. It happens very often: Operator STC gives you a hint, a prompt, and then you should formulate the **Ideal Final Result**, find the physical contradiction, use the rules of S-Field analysis and physics.

Let's try to use Operator STC in **Problem #41** about the roller conveyor. The diameter of the rolls will be smaller — about a hundred, or even a thousand, times smaller than that of a human hair. To build this conveyor is practically impossible. However, because we are doing a mental experiment, we should not be afraid of attempting it. Let's make the rollers as thin as molecules. We will stretch a molecule. The minimum thickness of a molecule is an atom, after that the molecule will break up. The melted glass ribbon will move over a layer of ball-atoms. This could be the best conveyor: ideally flat.

The prompt is given. Let's use it. Under the glass ribbon we should spread ball-atoms. These are not atoms of gas, because they can evaporate, and they are not atoms of hard matter, because they cannot move. The only possibility left is the atoms of a liquid. Glowing red, the glass ribbon rolls over a liquid surface! This is an ideal conveyor.

What kind of liquid could be chosen for this conveyor?

Let's not guess about that. Sherlock Homes, who perfectly understood the advantage of organized thinking, said once: "I never guess. That is a very bad habit, it kills the logical thinking process."

Let us take this statement into consideration, and let's look logically for the liquid that we need.

First of all, we need a liquid that melts easily. Second, this liquid should have a high boiling temperature, otherwise, when it boils, the glass surface will become wavy. The specific gravity of the liquid should be much higher than that of the gravity of the glass (2.5gr/cm3), otherwise, the glass ribbon will not stay on the surface of the liquid.

Hence, the liquid we are looking for should have the following properties: **Melting Temperature** no more than 200^0 - 300^0 C, **Boiling Temperature** no less than 1500^0 C, **Specific Gravity** no less than 5.0-6.0 gr/cm3.

Only metals have such properties. If we reject all rare metals for this purpose, what is left is bismuth, lead and tin. Bismuth is expensive. The vapor of lead is poisonous. What is left, is tin. The conclusion: Instead of a conveyor we will have a long tray with melted tin — atoms instead of thin rolls. The system has made a transition to a microlevel where a new development is available. In reality, after the patent was issued, many patents on improvements of that design were issued. For example, if we ran an electric current through melted tin we could change, with the use of magnets, the shape of the surface that will affect the surface of the glass. More than a hundred inventions were made utilizing this particular idea.

Below is a problem for you to solve with Operator STC.

Problem 44
A fresh idea is needed

A company had a very unusual project to develop for an oil pipeline. The same pipeline should be able to pump different liquid products alternately.

In order not to mix them, they have to be separated by a special device. After one liquid is pumped, a big ball used as a piston is inserted. Then another liquid is pumped.

"This device has no guarantee," said the manager of the project. "The pressure in the pipeline is great — tens of pounds. Liquids can seep by the ball and mix together."

"Maybe we should consider other devices to separate the liquids?" asked an engineer as he pulled out a catalog with disc type dividers. In the catalog there was a picture of a divider made out of three rubber discs.

"They get stuck very often," said the manager. "The main problem is that after every 200 km there is a pumping station. When the divider comes to the pumping station it should be removed, because it cannot get through the pump. Therefore disks and balls are no good. We need a divider that can go through the pump with a guarantee that the liquids will not mix."

And suddenly the inventor appeared.

"We can use Operator STC," he offered. "We need a fresh idea, don't we?"

And a fresh idea appeared. What kind of idea was it?

Apply the first question out of the six — decrease the size of the pipeline in your mind. Keep in mind that it is prohibited to make a horizontal separation. It is required that various liquids will flow through the pipeline alternately, without being mixed.

99

Chapter 24
A Crowd of Miniature Dwarfs

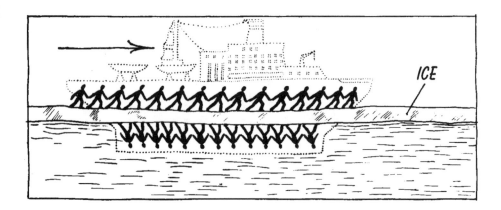

Operator STC is a very powerful tool, but not the only one that can help us to overcome psychological inertia. Psychological inertia can be carried by words, especially by technical terms. These terms exist in order to reflect very precisely what is known already. But an inventor has to get out of the known limits, and break away from the existing images created by those terms. Therefore, every problem should be restated by using "simple words."

In one of the seminars on the theory of solving inventive problems, the following happened. A sailor offered this task to be solved: How to increase the speed of an icebreaker going through the Arctic ice? This problem was solved by an engineer who had nothing to do with the construction of icebreakers, and he did it on the blackboard. There was the following note on the board: "A thing should freely pass through the ice, as if there were no ice at all."

I was sitting next to the sailor and heard his indignation: "He is a hooligan," he said. "Why does he call the icebreaker a thing?"

The engineer was correct in calling the icebreaker a "thing," because the word "icebreaker" imposed on you a notion that a ship had to break the ice. What if we can learn to get through the ice without breaking it? Therefore the term "thing" is very appropriate. It is the same as the "X" in mathematics.

By the way, the "thing" in reality is completely different from the icebreaker. Imagine a body of a ship that is built in such a way that the middle part disappears where the ice contacts the ship. Or, let us say, there is a ten-story building without a seventh floor. The body of the big icebreaker is like the ten story building. If one floor is removed, ice will pass through that floor freely, and the ship could move without breaking the ice (see picture above).

The ideal solution would be not to connect the upper and lower parts of the ship's body. But the practical solution should only be close to the ideal one. We have to step back a little from the ideal solution. We will connect both parts of the body with two very thin, strong, and sharp support-blades. They will cut a very narrow crack through the ice. It is much easier this way than to break the ice the whole width of the ship.

The problem was solved very artistically, but the sailor who offered the problem was not satisfied. At that time people made a lot of experiments to break ice by waterguns and so on. There were many inventions on the subject: "Let's break the ice." And of course, the "thing" that went through ice without breaking it did not fit into the overall picture. Six years later a patent was issued on a half submerged vessel. A new term had appeared. Then other patents came out. There are now **"Through-ice-ships"** being built in shipyards. As you can see, it takes a special imagination and knowledge of the evolution laws of technical systems in order to make the correct evaluation of an idea.

The method for overcoming psychological inertia that is used by **TRIZ** seems to be purely psychological. In reality, the purpose of that method is to show the direction of development of technical systems.

About thirty years ago an American engineer, William Gordon, offered to use an "empathy" method during the process of solving problems. The technique which that method employed was to make a person imagine himself as a machine in the system, living the life of that machine, trying to find a solution. This is a purely psychological method aiming to find new ways of looking at problems.

We decided to test this method, and we set up many experiments. It was found that "empathy" helped sometimes, but more often led to a dead end. When inventors imagine themselves as a machine they ignore ideas related to the destruction of that machine — separation of its parts, shredding, freezing, melting and so on. For a live organism, such actions are not acceptable. They are prohibited. Human beings, of course, transfer those notions to the machine — although the machine and its parts could be fragmented and crushed.

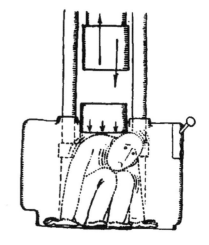

Take, for example, the problem about the roller conveyor. In searching for a solution we, in our mind, had to decrease the size of the rollers to atoms. The breaking up of parts is the main trend in the development of the working element of a machine. When parts are smaller, the control is easier, and the potential for machine improvement is greater. Take a look at the "Hovercraft" vehicle. The wheels are reduced to the size of gas molecules, the vehicle has become more mobile, and it can go over different terrains.

TRIZ uses miniature dwarfs instead of "empathy." The method is very simple. You should imagine that an object (machine, device) consists of a crowd of miniature dwarfs. Partially this reminds you of "empathy." You can look at the problem from the inside through the eyes of these dwarfs. This is "empathy" without "empathy." In our method, "empathy" has no defects. Ideas of reduction and breaking-up are accepted very easily. The crowd of miniature dwarfs could be separated and reorganized.

Once, as an experiment, a group of engineers were asked to work on the problem of the icebreaker by using the "empathy" method.

The engineers gladly offered various ideas about how to break the ice and how to break the icebreaker itself. After that, the same problem was given to another group of engineers and they were offered to use **Model with Miniature Dwarfs (MMD). This is Method #25.**

Several engineers offered similar ideas. Let the crowd of men (body of the ship) split and pass the ice (obstacle) on two sides. The group was new, and none of the people took this idea seriously.

"We are offering this idea as nonsense," said one of the engineers as an excuse.

MMD requires a very strong imagination. One should imagine that the object consists of many live, small thinking entities — not molecules or atoms. What do they feel? How do they act? How should they act? How should the crowd act? It is a very useful model for thinking if you have experience working with this model.

Problem 45
A capricious seesaw

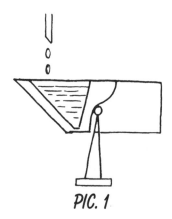

PIC. 1

A water batchmeter was made like a seesaw. (Pic.1.) There is a container for liquid on the left side of the batchmeter. The batchmeter tilts as soon as the container is filled with liquid. Then the liquid pours out of the container. Then the left side becomes lighter and the seesaw returns to balance. Unfortunately, the batchmeter does not work as accurately as necessary. Not all the liquid pours out of the container.

What happens is that as soon as the liquid starts to discharge from the container, the system starts to return to the empty balance position (the container

102

starts coming up), and we will thus have a "shortage" of poured liquid. What if we make the container bigger, and have an excess of liquid? We still will not reach the required accuracy and have the same "shortage" all the time because of many factors that we cannot control. The shortage should be eliminated by some other means.

Let's try to use method MMD. There are girls and boys on a seesaw. The girls are the "liquid" and the boys are the "counterweight." The load of liquid is accepted (Pic. 2), and the left side of the seesaw comes down (Pic.3). As soon as one or two girls jump off the seesaw, the left side starts to go up (Pic.4). What should be done so that all the girls get off the seesaw? The answer is that while the girls are coming off the seesaw, the boys should move closer to the center of the board (Pic.5). After all the girls have jumped off the seesaw, the boys can return to their original position (Pic.6).

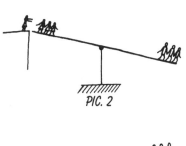

PIC. 2

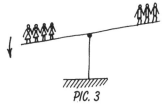

PIC. 3

Now we can go from the model to the real mechanism. A weight on the right side of the batcher has to slide easily from left to right. It is clear that a weight in the form of a ball is the most appropriate in our case (Pic.7).

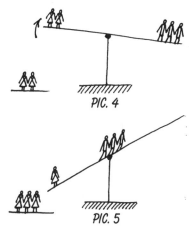

PIC. 4

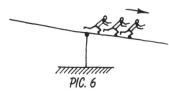

PIC. 5

PIC. 6

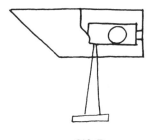

PIC. 7

The problem is solved. We got the answer by using Method MMD. It is not difficult to notice that the technical contradiction was discovered and removed. The moment of the force acting on the right side of the seesaw should be small, so that the liquid could pour out of the container, and should be big enough so that the liquid could fill the container. We can say that the batcher which did not have moving parts has now become "dynamic." This means the system has entered the Third Period of its development. Therefore, everything

103

was done correctly, and the solution is a very good one.

Problem 46
Contrary to physics

If one spins a container full of liquid, the centrifugal force will press the liquid against the container's wall. This phenomenon is used very often for the treatment of different products under pressure. Suppose that the item is placed not on the walls of the container, but in the center of the container (Pic.1). How, in this case, can we force the liquid to press the object? That goes against the law of physics.

Let us use method MMD. The physical contradiction here is that the "liquid-men" should press the object (Pic.2), but, by the laws of physics, they have to press onto the opposite side — the wall (Pic.3). We are now going to work this problem out as TRIZ suggests.

We will try to superimpose that which is not superimposable. Let's assume that we have two opposite actions at the same time (Pic.4).

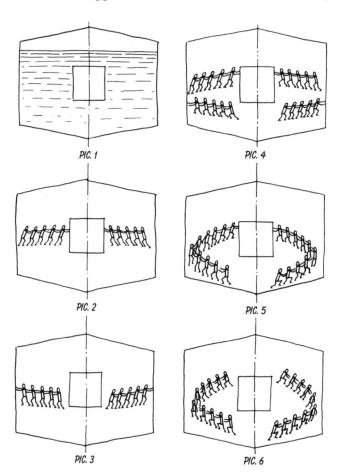

PIC. 1   PIC. 4

PIC. 2   PIC. 5

PIC. 3   PIC. 6

104

Unfortunately, the "small men" press only against the walls and do not press against the object. This means that the pressure to the wall should reversed direction (Pic.5). How can we do this? If we send one row of "men" against another, we can neutralize the action (Pic.6), the same as when two teams pull a rope on opposite ends and the forces are even. However, nothing prevents us from having heavier and stronger "men" in the bottom row (Pic.7). This is the answer.

Let us have two liquids in a vessel, for instance, oil and Mercury (Pic.8). During the spin of the vessel, the mercury overcomes the pressure of the oil and the oil will press against the object. This is a wonderful solution for a problem that seemed to be unsolvable.

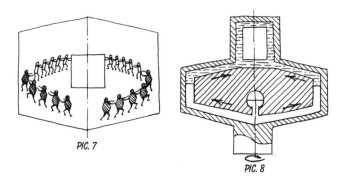

PIC. 7

PIC. 8

Now try to find a solution to **Problem #44** about the pipeline separator. Imagine yourself as a separator. A group of "blue men" separates the flow of "red men" into two parts. How should the "blues" act during transportation inside the pipeline? What characteristics should the "blues" have in order to get through the pumps? How should the "blues" behave after the trip is over and they are in the same tank with the "reds?"

105

Chapter 25
The Ideal Machine is No Machine

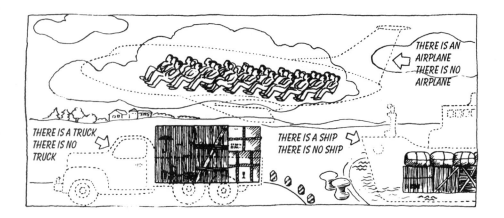

Heavy, rugged, inflexible systems should be replaced by light, "airlike," even ephemeral systems built from small particles, molecules, atoms, ions, or electrons controlled by different fields. An ideal machine should not have a heavy weight or a large volume. **The Ideal Machine is when an action is completed and there is no machine.** Therefore, the definition of the Ideal Final Result is based on the utilization of the main laws of the system's technical evolution. At the same time it is a psychological method. When one is oriented to IFR, one is not thinking any more about the old shape of the machine. The transition to IFR is a very powerful procedure, that allows you to formulate IFR very precisely. At this point, let us not get into too much detail. The main thing is to demand that everything should be done by itself, just like in a fairy tale.

Problem 47
Like in a fairy tale

There was a discussion about a new hothouse on a certain farm. "Overall it is not bad," said the director. "But there is no automation! Look at the roof of the hothouse. It is a light metal frame with a glass, or film, hinged on one side. If the temperature inside goes higher then 20^0 C, we will have to lift the frame; if it is less than 20^0 C, we will have to close the roof. During the daytime the temperature in the hothouse could change ten times. We cannot open and close the roof by hand all the time."

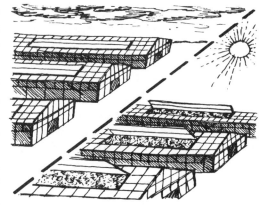

"Why by hand?" said the mechanic. "We can put in a special device, like a temperature relay. When a temperature change occurs, that will turn the motor on. We will design a special gear to connect the motor and the frame."

"That is not acceptable," resolutely said the accountant. "We have hundreds of hothouses, and if every one will have this mechanism it will be very complicated and costly."

"We have a technical contradiction," summarized the director. "We gain in automation, but we lose in complexity and cost of the hothouse."

And suddenly the inventor appeared.

"Let's formulate IFR," he said. "It should be like in a fairy tale. A good formulation of IFR plus knowledge of tenth grade physics, and the problem is solved."

How do we formulate IFR for this particular problem? What did the inventor have in mind when he mentioned tenth grade physics?

Let's look at this problem together. First of all, notice that this is not a problem , this is a situation out of which we have to "extract" the problem.

The system "hothouse" is very young, it has not yet become a "dynamic," "flexible" system. Therefore, the task is to preserve the hothouse *as it is*, trying not to change it, but *eliminate its shortcomings*. The roof is not moveable, and the plants are overheated. We will not even consider mechanizing the hothouse at all, because the electric motor and gears are a completely new system. IFR should be like this: **"The roof opens up by itself as the temperature rises, and closes down as the temperature drops."**

An inexperienced person will say: "It is impossible!" But we know very well that this type of "miracle" is possible.

In **Problem #32** about the protection of the power lines, the ferromagnetic rings obtained and lost magnetic properties by themselves. Why can't we make a "contract" with our roof, so the roof will go up and down? Just as the thermofield controls ferromagnetic rings, let it control our roof. This means that we can use the thermal expansion of material. Let's take a rod and.... No, nothing will come of it. The rod will expand only one tenth of one percent even in a high temperature. That is exactly why we used that characteristic for micromovements. In our case we have to create a movement of 20-30 cm.

If we look into the physics textbook we will find a chapter about bimetallic plates: two metal strips are connected together — copper and iron. Copper expands more rapidly than iron when heated. In the bimetallic plate those strips connected together bend a lot under the application of heat. A hothouse roof made with these strips will go up when the temperature increases, and down when the temperature decreases.

Problem 48
Ships of the 21st Century

In a certain design firm a team of engineers was working on improving a power-driven barge. The work was really boring. There was nothing new in the project. A barge is a barge: add a more powerful engine, get more speed — that was it.

"Why can't we try to develop a ship for the 21st Century?" the youngest engineer said. "Everything will be completely new in it."

"Even the body?" his friend asked.

"Even the body!" answered the engineer. "The body is the first to be changed, because it has not been changed for thousands of years. It used to be wooden, now it is made of steel."

"What is the difference? It is still a box," said the third engineer.

"The body always will be a box," somebody added.

And suddenly the inventor appeared.

"Do not argue," he said. "The theory of solving inventive problems should be used. Nowadays, the body of a ship has the shape of a streamlined box made out of steel. This technical system is in the second period of its development. This means that it needs to make a transition to a flexible body. Maybe it needs to make a transition from macrolevel to microlevel — build the ship out of atoms and molecules controlled by a field. We can set a more courageous task for ourselves. The ideal machine is when there is no machine, but the action is done. This means that the ideal body is when there is no body, but the ship exists, works, moves, and so on. Let's try to make a model out of minuscule dwarfs and Operator STC."

Hence, imagine the wall of the ship. There is a thick steel plate. Now replace it with a crowd of minuscule dwarfs. What should be done in order to keep those dwarfs together under the impact of the waves? How should these dwarfs act in order to increase the speed of the ship? The conventional wall has a lot of friction with water and slows down the movement. But when you have a wall of dwarfs, you can command them, and they will do anything you say.

Play with the dwarfs (try to build a mental model of a new wall). Then turn back to real technology. How, in the real world, can we do what these dwarfs are doing?

When you solve this task, go to the next one. How should the ship look, having an ideal body? Here you have to use Operator STC. Suppose the size of the ship is equal to a molecule. In reality the ship does not exist. There is a molecule, the cargo is an atom. How will this molecule transport an atom? Imagine this picture, and carry this concept over to the real ship. It has to be as though there is a body and there is no body....

Part 5
The Algorithm of Talent

Chapter 26
The Suit for Portos

When you see a town for the first time some things strike your eyes and some things are missed. The same thing happens with our excursion into TRIZ. After reading over everything written, I found nothing said about several interesting methods. In order to get a better feeling for these methods, we will begin with a problem.

Problem 49
The train will leave in five minutes

Big wooden logs are loaded onto open railroad cars. An inspector measures the diameter of each log in order to calculate the volume of the load. This work progresses very slowly. "We have to hold the train," the chief inspector said. "We cannot finish today."

And suddenly, of course, the inventor appeared.

"I have an idea!" he exclaimed. "The train can leave in five minutes. Take..."

And he explained what should be taken, and what needed to be done. What can you offer?

When this problem was published in the youth magazine *Pioneer Truth*, correct answers were received from those children who remembered that a technical contradiction should be removed in order to solve a technical problem.

Here are some of the incorrect answers:

• Let this work be done by a team of 300 - 500 people.

• Determine visually the average diameter of one log, and count how many of them are on the car.

• Cut cross-sections of all the logs, then accurately measure their diameters after the train has left.

To gain in accuracy, one needs to pay the price of complicating the system. And vice versa — simplify a measurement and you lose accuracy. Behind this technical contradiction the physical one is hidden — the train should leave the station, and the train should not leave the station.

"Something" has to be done to enable the train to leave and still remain. We can formulate a new inventive method: If it is difficult to measure the object itself, a copy should be made, and then that copy can be measured. **This is Method #26: Make a copy and work with it.**

In a couple of minutes one can take a photo of all the logs from the back of the car. A measuring stick is attached to the logs as a reference scale before the photo is taken. Then the train can go. All measurements can be made from the photo.

It is interesting that the first person to describe this idea was Alexander Dumas, the author of *The Three Musketeers*. There is a chapter in his book, *Ten Years Later*, describing how Portos ordered a new suit from a tailor. Portos would not agree to let the tailor touch him when taking his measurements. The playwright Moliere, who was in the hall of the tailor's shop at that time, found a way out of this situation. Moliere brought Portos up to the mirror and took his measurements from the mirror image.

There are many clever methods we could discuss at length. But, being a visitor in town for the first time, it is enough to view some typical buildings, walk through a few typical streets, and examine a map of the town.

Now you are familiar with several laws of the development of technical systems, and know about two dozen methods. I hope you even know how to use some of the physical phenomena. Of course this is only one section of the town called TRIZ, but this is a typical one. Let us now look at a map of TRIZ and see how everything appears in a complete, unified system.

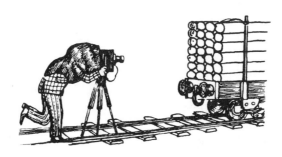

Chapter 27
Let's Build a Model of a Problem

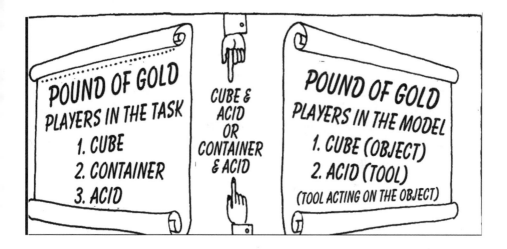

The first **"Algorithm" of solving inventive problems — ARIZ** (the Russian acronym) — was developed thirty years ago. The word "algorithm" means a program of sequential actions. In math classes you work with algorithms very often. Algorithms can be found everywhere. Let's take the rule for crossing a highway. First you look to the left and, if there are no cars, you go. After reaching the middle of the highway, you look to the right, then go.

In the first chapter of this book, I said you need a bridge to get from the problem to the answer. **ARIZ is that bridge**. There are seven steps in ARIZ. Every step consists of several sub-steps. The total number of steps is about fifty, with every step containing several different operations. There are rules that help avoid mistakes while going from step to step. These rules can be compared to the handrails of a bridge. There is a list comprising the main steps and methods, as well as tables on how to use physical effects. This is a complex system, not just simply rules for asking: "What will happen if I do this?"

Part 1 of ARIZ is the formulation of the task.

You already know something about this. We discussed the question of when should a problem be solved (*modernize the existing system*), and when a system should be replaced (*find something completely new*). The operator **STC** is part of the first chapter of ARIZ. We have not yet discussed another important step — how to use **Standards**.

Together with simple steps, there are also complex methods consisting of several simple steps. Simple steps are universal; indeed, they can be used to solve a large variety of problems. The more complex the method, the more it is connected with a specific class of problems. There is great power in complex methods, and the combination of methods brings interesting and unusual solutions that are very close to the Ideal Final Result. The most powerful of the complex methods are called **Standards.**

We are already familiar with one of the Standards. In order to move, compress, stretch, fragment — in other words, control — a substance (and that substance will not be destroyed by the introduction of additives) one can add ferromagnetic particles controlled by a magnetic field.

The first part of ARIZ suggests analyzing the problem in order to determine whether or not it can be solved by using one of the Standards. If a problem is typical, there is no need to go through all the steps of ARIZ. It is much easier to use the appropriate Standard. There are more than 80 Standards.

This chapter helps to screen typical problems, and change non-typical problems — or re-define them. Then "mushy" or "foggy" situations become precisely stated problems.

In the second part of ARIZ, the transition is made from the *problem* to a *model of the problem.*

There are many players (parts of the system) in a problem. In the model of the problem, there are only two players. The conflict between them is a *technical contradiction*. Very often the model of the problem consists of the object itself and the environment surrounding the object. You probably remember **Problem #40** about the clinker. The object is hot clinker, and the environment is the cool air contacting its surface.

In a situation or in a task, we talk about the whole technical system — but in a model, we consider only two parts of the system. There is hot melted clinker and a column of cold air above it. That is the whole model! The blast furnaces, railroad stations, and even the containers are not included in the model. There are only two conflicting parts left — and that is a significant step forward. The discarded parts are worthless variants that would have to otherwise be analyzed.

There are rules in ARIZ on how to build a model of a problem. A model always should have a **Product** and a **Tool** (an instrument that works on the product and changes it). **This is Method #27: Build a model of the problem**

The correct determination of the conflicting pair of elements very often brings an immediate solution to the problem. Let's see how it works in a simple problem.

Problem 50
A pound of gold

In a small scientific laboratory, scientists study the effects of hot acid on various alloys. In a container with thick steel walls, 15 - 20 cubes of different alloys are placed. Acid is poured on them. The chamber is then closed and an electric oven turned on. This test lasts between one and two weeks. The samples are then removed and their surfaces studied under a microscope.

"It is very bad," said the manager of the laboratory one day. "Acid has corroded the walls of the container."

"We should put in some kind of lining," offered one of the workers in the lab. "Maybe we should use gold?"

"Or platinum," said another worker.

"It will not work," the manager responded. "We will gain stability in the chamber but lose in cost. I have already calculated that it will take about one pound of gold...."

And suddenly the inventor appeared.

"Why do we have to use gold?" he said. "Let us look at a model of the problem, and automatically we will get another solution."

How do you build a model of the problem?

First, let us examine the problem. There is a *system* here. The system consists of three parts — the chamber, the acid and the alloy cubes. Usually, people think that the problem is to prevent the chamber walls from being corroded by the acid. This means that you are forced to consider the conflict between the chamber and the acid, so naturally everyone tries to protect the walls from the acid. Can you imagine what happens? A small laboratory that is studying alloys should now drop all projects and start to solve a very complex problem that thousands of scientists have helplessly worked on in the past: How to protect steele from corrosion. Suppose that this problem will finally be solved — it will take time, maybe years. The alloy test has to be done today, not tomorrow.

Let's use the rules of model building. The *product* is the cubes being tested. The acid acts on the cubes. That's it — our model of the problem. The chamber does not fit in the model. The only conflict to be considered is that between the cubes and the acid.

Here is where the most interesting thing happens. Acid corrodes the walls of the chamber. We understand the conflict between the chamber and the acid. In our model we only have cubes and acid. Where is the conflict between them? Where is the problem now? Acid corrodes the walls of the cubes. Let it corrode! This is the goal of the test. This means that *there is no conflicting situation.*

In order to understand the essence of the conflict, we have to remember that we did not include the chamber in our model. The acid should stay next to the cubes without the chamber. The acid by itself cannot do that. It will spread all over the place.

This is the conflict that needs to be removed. We have replaced the very complicated task of preventing corrosion with the very simple task of preventing the acid touching the cubes from spreading or spilling.

The answer is clear without further analysis. The cube should be made hollow as a cup, and then the acid poured inside the cube.

F_{GR}

S_2 S_1

We can arrive at the same answer by using S-Field analysis. Gravity field Fgr changes the shape of the acid S_1 (forcing it to spread) and does not change the shape of the cube S_2.

There is no S-Field. It lacks one connection, one arrow.

There may be only two variants:

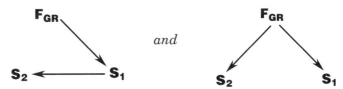

The first variant is when the acid transfers its weight to the cube and presses against it. For that, the acid should be poured into the cube.

The second variant is when the acid and the cube have the same influence on the gravity field. There is a free fall of the acid and the cube. Under such conditions the acid will not separate from the cube. Theoretically this is the correct answer. Yet practically, for the purpose of our problem, this is a very complicated system.

Note that guessing gave you one answer while analysis "caught" two.

Yes, Sherlock Holmes rejected guessing with good reason!

There is no S-Field. It lacks one connection, one arrow.

There may be only two variants:

The first variant is when the acid transfers its weight to the cube and presses against it. For that, the acid should be poured into the cube.

The second variant is when the acid and the cube have the same influence on the gravity field. There is a free fall of the acid and the cube. Under such conditions the acid will not separate from the cube. Theoretically this is the correct answer. Yet practically, for the purpose of our problem, this is a very complicated system.

Note that guessing gave you one answer while analysis "caught" two.

Yes, Sherlock Holmes rejected guessing with good reason!

Chapter 28
Familiar Trick: There is a Substance, and There is No Substance

Thus, **Part 1 of ARIZ** is designed to formulate the given problem.

Part 2 of ARIZ is designed to make a transition from the problem to a model.

Part 3 of ARIZ is designed to make an analysis of that model. First, determine which element of the conflicting pair should be changed. There are certain rules for this. The "Tool" should be changed. Only if it is impossible to change the "Tool" by the conditions of the task should the outside environment be changed.

The next step is the formulation of the **IFR** (**Ideal Final Result**). For example: "Acid sticks to the cube by itself." If the answer to the "cube problem" was not quite clear before, it should be clear now. This is a very simple task. We used it only as an example. In more complicated problems the analysis must be more extensive. It should be determined what section of the model cannot comply with the requirements stated in the **IFR**, and then we can formulate the physical contradiction.

Look what will happen:

First, we have to deal with an Inventive Situation in which several technical systems are included.

Then we move from this Inventive Situation to the Inventive Problem, choosing only one technical system.

We then build a model of the problem, taking only a section of the system (two elements of it).

Finally, we choose one element and its operating zone that needs to be changed.

With each step the area of search gets narrower. Diagnosis determines the sick area — "the surgery should be done here."

The "sickness" is diagnosed. In Inventive Situations we have only common complaints: *This* is bad, inconvenient, too expensive, and so on. From the diagnosis we make a transition first to the **Technical Contradiction** then to the **Physical Contradiction**.

As soon as we determine the **Physical Contradiction** and the "sick" area, the analysis is considered complete.

For example, take **Problem 40** about the clinker. We already know how to make the transition from a Situation to a Problem. Everything was left without any changes, but there is no longer a cold crust on the clinker. We have already discussed the model of that problem: Hot melted clinker surrounded by cold air. Now, clinker is a *product*. This means that we have to work with the surrounding air. The **IFR** states that cold air should prevent the clinker from cooling off. This seems, at first, a pretty wild thought. The cold air should protect the clinker from the — cold air!

Let's continue. What area of air cannot comply with the **IFR** requirement? Probably, that zone directly in contact with the surface of the hot clinker. Now we can see a **Physical Contradiction**. That area of cold air directly above the clinker should contain something to hold the heat, while at the same time be empty in order to allow the clinker to be loaded and unloaded.

Hence, a special layer of some substance should be above the surface of the clinker, and at the same time it should not be there. We have already solved similar problems.

You may remember a special rule: **In those cases where we cannot add any foreign substance, we can add a modification of an existing one as a third substance**.

In our case we have only the clinker and air, therefore there are only three answers:

1. **Use modified air**. Heat the layer of air that has immediate contact with the clinker. This is a bad solution. It requires installing special burners that pollute the atmosphere.

2. **Use a modified clinker**. Cover the surface of the liquid clinker with small balls made out of light, hard clinker. This will be good insulation; however, it will introduce many inconveniences. The balls must be manufactured, and something must hold them inside the container during the discharge of melted clinker.

3. **Use a mixture of clinker and air**. Mix air and clinker to obtain — foam. This is an excellent insulator! Pour the clinker into the container and make a layer of foam that will be a great insulator and a good cover. It will be easy to pour out clinker without paying attention to the cover. Liquid clinker will get through this lid easily. There *is* a lid and there *is no* lid.

117

The problem is solved in principle. What is left is just the technical matter of how to make the foam. The simplest method is to add a little water during the process of filling the container with clinker. Notice the paradox: *In order to preserve heat, the clinker is sprayed with cold water.* That water, interacting with hot clinker, will produce the clinker foam.

This problem was first solved with ARIZ by the inventor Michael Sharapov of Magnitogorsk, USSR. His invention was implemented at once by many metallurgical plants.

The answer to the problem with the clinker is surprisingly simple. I have no doubt that you can appreciate the "beauty" of it.

Logical steps, and directions of thought, are probably the most complicated things. I recommend re-reading these pages. Follow how we moved from the situation to the problem, and finally to the model — how the **IFR** and the physical contradiction were formulated — and how we searched for the substance that both *existed* and *did not exist* at the same time. This is a small fragment of ARIZ, but if you understand step by step how the task is worked out, then you have gotten the meaning of ARIZ and this book has not been read in vain.

Chapter 29
If The Problem is Stubborn

In 800 AD, the Roman Pope had to crown Carl the Great. This was a serious problem. On one hand, it was necessary for the Pope to place the crown on Carl's head; however, in the eyes of subordinates, this meant that Carl became the lawful Emperor with the Church's official consent. On the other hand, this could not be permitted because it would mean that Carl would get his power from the Pope — and the Pope could also take it back.

The problem, as you can see, is a typical inventive one — and Carl the Great found the correct solution. The coronation sermon was going smoothly. When the Pope lifted the crown to place it on Carl's head, Carl took the crown from the Pope's hands and placed it on his head himself. So, half way the crown was in the Pope's hands, and the other half it was in Carl's hands. The contradictory requirements were separated in space and time. At the beginning, the coronation was in the hands of the Pope. At the end, it was in the hands of Carl.

The fourth part of ARIZ was designed precisely to remove this type of contradiction.

Method 28: Separation of contradictory requirements in time and/or in space.

The analysis of problems does not always lead to answers, even when done precisely. Very often it happens that a contradiction is determined and formulated, but the means of removing it remains unknown. In the first part of ARIZ, means to combat the contradiction were collected.

At first, simple tools are offered — like those that separate contradictory requirements in time and space. If the contradiction cannot be solved, then more complex tools should be used from the table of S-Field transformations. By that time, the kinds of substances and fields the model of the problem is built with should be known. Then it is not so difficult to draw an S-Field diagram, and the table shows how to transform the diagram to get our answer. If the problem still cannot be solved, the fourth part of ARIZ offers one more tool: **A Table of Physical Effects and Phenomena**. It also reveals in which cases the table should be used.

Suppose we have difficulty in solving **Problem 37** — how to replace the microscrew. In the Table we look in the section "Micromovements." There we find three physical effects — thermal expansion, opposite piezoeffect, and magnetostriction. We can then open a reference book to get more details on these effects.

What if the problem continues to be stubborn? Then the last reserve is used: **The Table of Typical Methods and Principles.**

In order to develop this table, over forty thousand patents were analyzed. Only very strong patents were selected. The table shows what kind of methods can be used to remove technical contradictions. In essence, this table reflects the experience of several generations of inventors. It shows you how inventors solved problems that were similar to yours.

If one feels that the problem is still not solved, then somewhere in the beginning there was a mistake. One should go back to Part 1 of ARIZ.

After the problem is solved, the work is still not finished. A careful step-by-step analysis of the solution is performed in order to yield solutions to new problems. This is **Part 5 of ARIZ.** Then the *development of found solutions* begins and is used toward solving other problems. This is **Part 6 of ARIZ**.

For example, the idea of a protective layer made out of foam in the clinker problem can be used again in **Problem 39** (the transportation of coal by conveyor belt). Let's cover the ore on the conveyor with a layer of foam to eliminate the dust. It's easy, and the foam will also not interfere with unloading the conveyor — an excellent solution.

Part 7 of ARIZ is a self-check. Here one compares the actual procedure used in solving the problem with that offered by ARIZ. Were there deviations? Why? Did ARIZ have flaws in its steps? Why? Can we add to the list of standards the new one found?

In schools and seminars on ARIZ, hundreds of written solutions are analyzed every year. These notes allow us to determine what mistakes were made by the students and/or by ARIZ. Such mistakes are studied carefully, and corrections are entered into the system of ARIZ. At the beginning I compared ARIZ with a town. Now we can say that ARIZ is a town where the construction of new buildings is a continuous process. Small new blocks are built, old blocks are rebuilt, and new roads are constructed.

Chapter 30
How to Become a Master

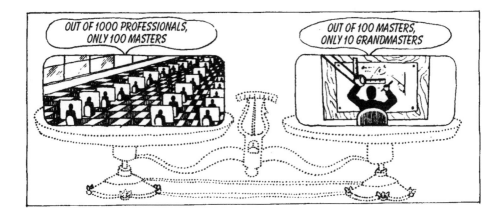

OUT OF 1000 PROFESSIONALS, ONLY 100 MASTERS

OUT OF 100 MASTERS, ONLY 10 GRANDMASTERS

Very often I have had to answer the question: "How can I become an inventor?" Sometimes people say: "Please look at my project and tell me whether or not I can be an inventor." The projects are usually very weak, but this has no bearing on an ability to become an inventor.

When I was in the fourth grade an idea struck me: "What would happen if a blimp was made with a vacuum inside? After all, the lighter the gas inside the blimp, the more force there would be to lift it up."

A very brilliant idea came out of that conclusion: If inside the blimp a complete vacuum could be developed, then the lifting force would be greatest. I never realized that, in this case, atmospheric pressure would crush the blimp!

So, how to become an inventor?

This is not different from how to become a writer, a surgeon, a pilot, and so on.

Anyone can become a professional in any type of activity in general. First, one has to get an education, then graduate from college. There are institutions for most professions. If this is a new profession, one must educate oneself. How did a person become a motion picture cameraman in, let us say, 1910? By independently learning this new profession through practice. How did a person become a professional in rocket technology in 1930? Again, independently studying the subject from books, and practicing with other groups of interested people. At the end of 1950 the science of technology forecasting was formed. Where did such professional people come from? All of them had come from other professions — engineers, economists, historians and so on.

I want to emphasize that anyone can become a professional — you just have to learn the subject matter. That's it. Out of the thousands of people who graduate from high school, probably all can become professionals. In reality, this not true. And, from a thousand professionals, only one hundred may become Master of their profession.

Again, I must emphasize that, in general, everyone can become a Master. In reality, one out of ten do so because of the high price it costs in labor. Professionals study hard for five or six years — and sometimes ten years. A Master learns all his life. A professional works seven or eight hours a day — maybe nine or ten. A Master works all the time. Sometimes people say: "Look at him! How talented he is! Everything he does seems so easy." This is a ridiculous statement because **talent is 99 percent hard work**.

What then?

Then, out of ten Masters, only one will become a "Grandmaster." Here, not everything depends on the person. First of all, demand for the "Grandmaster's" product needs to emerge from society. Someone first needs to order a unique building from a "Master-Architect" providing the necessary challenge for that Master to stretch and grow to "Grandmaster." There are also other outside factors. The area of the Master's activity should have potentials for development. In the 19th Century there were many great Masters who designed and built sailing ships. But the Grandmaster of shipbuilding soon became a watchmaker and a painter when the inventor Robert Fulton built the unpretentious steamboat.

When one asks how to become an inventor, what one really has in mind is how to become a Master — or even Grandmaster. Now you know the answer. First, you have to become a professional. Anyone can accomplish that. Then, we will see....

As yet there are no learning institutions to teach how to become an inventor. But, there are many seminars, courses, schools and public institutions in Russia today that teach inventive creativity. However, this book is enough for you to get started.

Much useful information is published in different magazines in Russia. Articles on different physical, chemical, and geometrical effects create an interest among readers. A special page in the magazine *Pioneer Truth* is called "To Invent? It is *so* difficult! It is *so* simple!" This is very useful. The meaning of the title is clear. It is difficult to invent without having knowledge of inventive methods. It is much easier with that knowledge. The purpose of *Pioneer Truth*'s page is to create a competition and an interest in creative thinking among readers. They can get all the help they want. Winners get prizes, books and other gifts.

Below are six problems from that magazine. Try your ability. If you can solve four out of six, you have a good chance of winning.

Problem 51
The secret of a sleuth dog

An employee at the Byelorussian Technological Institute recently got Patent #791389 on a toy — a sleuth dog. The dog moves among plastic sticks lying on the floor. Suddenly it stops next to one of the sticks and starts to "bark." It is not difficult to understand how the toy moves on the floor. There is a battery, an electric motor, and wheels. It is also easy to understand how it barks. There is a battery, a small speaker, and so on. The trick is to find out how the dog can find one specific stick out of many. A real dog does it by sniffing the object. But the toy should do it differently. What kind of invisible mark can be placed on that stick, and how can the dog detect it. If you find it difficult to get the answer, look at a seventh grade physics textbook.

Problem 52
Dangerous planet

A very unusual Planet was described in a fiction story. Everything on that planet was similar to our Planet Earth except that the birds and insects flew at supersonic speeds. We are not going to clarify how they did this. The essence of the story is that it was very dangerous to encounter such creatures. They could kill you like a bullet. So, the air is filled with "flying bullets" and "shells." Two cosmonauts disembarked from their spaceship and were nearly killed. Even an armored vehicle was destroyed by these supersonic "flies." Can you imagine being a member of an expedition on that planet?

Offer safety measures for the cosmonauts.

Problem 53
Icicles in roof gutters and downspouts

In spring a lot of snow collects in gutters and downspouts. During the day, it melts partially and at night freezes again. Slowly but surely, a huge ice plug is developed inside the spout. The length of that plug sometimes reaches several meters. This plug is held tight inside by attaching itself to the inner wall of the spout. On spring days the sun heats the spout melting the surface of the huge icicle. Finally it falls down, breaking the bend in the spout. Splinters of that icicle can fly out from the spout and hurt pedestrians.

You have to find a way to prevent downspouts from being damaged, and pedestrians from being hurt when the spout icicles fall down.

Problem 54
A drop of paint is the main hero

Once upon a time, the inventor B. Travkin discovered that when a drop of tooth-cleaning liquid is put on the surface of water it develops a "moving flower" effect. In order to better see this effect, the inventor added black ink to the tooth cleaner. This is how the invention called Fokaj started. Fokaj is the Russian abbreviation of "the patterns developed from contacts between active liquids."

It is easy to make a motion picture by using Fokaj. For instance, a thin layer of yellow liquid is poured into a glass pan. Then one drop of a blue liquid is added. On the border between blue and yellow a green ring appears. The drop spreads slowly, mixes with more liquid, the colors change, and a freakish play of color suddenly appears. The glass pan is lighted and the camera starts. It looks like a scene from another planet, lighted by a "blue sun." Fokaj is very appealing, because ordinary liquids can be used: varnish, glycerin, liquid soap, ink and glue. At the same time Fokaj has one shortcoming. It is impossible to control the movement of the drops and the play of colors. The camera operator has to interrupt shooting and make corrections with a brush and a stick. This is too cumbersome. Our goal is to control the drop movements from the bottom of the pan during the photographing of the scene.

For instance, the cameraman has to make a movie depicting ball lightning. The pan is filled with blue liquid two-to-three millimeters deep. This will be the sky. We add one drop of orange liquid. The drop falls down to the bottom of the pan. Around the drop a color crown appears. So far everything is fine. We now have ball lightning. The problem is how to control the movement of that crown. The ball lightning should spin and have a spiral movement — or take some other path. Ball lightning sometimes splits-up. How can we split our drop? How can we show the explosion?

You can see now how simple the problem is. How can we find a way to control the motion of the drop without a brush or a stick?

Problem 55
We can manage the droplets

A testing device was assembled in one of the laboratories. A very important test had to be performed with polymers. This device has a vertical tube, inside of which a droplet of polymer has to fall. The device was turned on and....

"Turn it off," said the supervisor of the laboratory. "It's no good. We need small droplets, and what we have now are only large drops."

"Only large droplets could be made," said the engineer. "There is nothing we can do."

"We have to break up the drops while they are falling," objected the supervisor. "I do not know how to do that.... Install a screen? No, that's no good either. The droplets shouldn't have any obstacles in their fall."

And suddenly the inventor appeared.

"Don't worry, we can manage the droplets," he said. "We have one substance. Let's add another substance and a field. It is very simple. The field will act on the second substance to break down drops into droplets while they fly."

Problem 56
A and B were sitting on a pipe

There are two devices — *A* and *B* — connected by a steel pipe. Usually device *A* has a higher temperature then device *B*. The pipe is heated, and the heat radiates through the walls of the pipe from *A* to *B* (similar to heat from hot tea radiating through the cup into the handle). Sometimes the temperature in device *B* sharply increases. Heat should not move from *B* to *A*. What can be done with the pipe so that the heat is conducted only in one direction — from *A* to *B*?

Part 6

The Amazing World of Tasks

Chapter 31
It Takes Wit

Technical problems must be solved in all areas of human activity. The foundation of these problems is always the removal of contradictions. In time, a theory for solving problems will be developed in science, art, and the administrative activities of society. Individual theories will slowly blend into a "Common Theory of Creative Thinking." This may happen in 20 to 30 years. Today we must perfect our Creative Thinking process by solving inventive problems.

We can start with problems that require only our minds and some thought. These problems do not require any specialized knowledge of physics. They can be solved by sixth grade students who need only think a little.

Problem 57
The hunter and the dog

Once there was an old hunter who brought his dog hunting in the forest. The dog barked when it found its prey, and the hunter walked toward the sound. But disaster struck when the hunter lost his hearing. In order to find its prey, the dog must be free and not kept close to the hunter. But, since the hunter couldn't hear the dog barking, the dog must stay close enough to be within the hunter's sight. This is a contradiction!

And suddenly the inventor....

No! In this story the inventor did not appear. The old hunter starved for many days trying to think of what to do. Finally he found the solution.

Let us try to solve the problem. First we have to draw a diagram of the conditions of the problem: "Dog" S_1 (Arrow 1) develops an acoustical field — barks (F_{AC}).

Field F_{AC} acts on "Hunter's ears" S_2 (Arrow 2). The hunter walks toward the dog — S_1 (Arrow 3).

Now we have an S-Field, and everything is fine..

When the hunter lost his hearing, he couldn't hear the dog barking. The field, F_{ac}, still exists but does not act on the hunter (see the far right line on the drawing below).

The S-Field is now destroyed: F_{ac} is not acting on S_2, and therefore S_2 is not moving towards S_1. What can we do?

Of course, it is not acceptable to keep the dog next to the hunter. It is not acceptable either to offer a hearing aid. The old hunter does not have that kind of help.

In solving this problem avoid using the "Trial and Error" method. This problem is homework. You can find the answer in the book Evil Spirit of Yambooh by G. Fedoseyev.

Problem 58
There are alibis, but....

The following story appeared in an issue of the magazine *World of Adventures*: One night two people were killed. One was the gangster Morgan, and the other was a scientist, Leo Lanser. In the first murder case the suspect was Morgan's competing gangster, Foyt. In the second case the suspect was professor Graycher. However, each suspect submitted proof of their alibis. In the end the prosecutor convicted both suspects. The question is: How could they both have committed crimes and yet still have proven alibis?

Problem 59
The arrow of Robin Hood

Robin Hood raised his bow and fired. An arrow flew through the air toward the sheriff's scout.

"He missed again!" exclaimed the film director. "Two meters higher than the target! We have a champion archer as a stuntman, and nothing is going right."

"Let's make a composite scene," offered the cameraman. "We will take three different shots. First, the bow and then the flying arrow. Robin Hood will then move within three meters of the scout and I will make the final shot. I hope that from a distance of three meters he can hit the target. Then we will make a montage of the clips and be finished."

"Never!" the producer shouted. "The audience knows this trick too well. The scene should be shot continuously. Robin Hood releases the arrow. The arrow flies and strikes the scout in the heart. Everyone should see that Robin Hood made the shot from a distance. We need reality."

"Then you will have to make the movie without me," said the actor playing the role of the scout, and he pulled a piece of plywood from his jacket pocket. "Robin Hood himself could never hit his target from that distance. This is terrible! I must concentrate on acting, but instead I have to think about what happens if the arrow is off just a little bit...."

The stuntman playing Robin Hood walked over and spread his arms with a guilty face. "I never worried during the Olympic games as much as I do now. I raise the bow at the last moment because I'm afraid I'll shoot the actor."

"Tomorrow the weather will not be right," the cameraman said. "It's best to finish this scene today."

And the Inventor appeared.

"We can do it today," he said. "We just need a little trick, and the arrow will hit the spot with the wooden plate."

In half an hour the shooting continued and the scene was finished without complications. What do you think the Inventor offered?

Let's try to clarify the conditions of the problem: Combined shots were not allowed. Robin Hood was standing far from the scout, and the audience must see the arrow fly and hit the scout. In the jacket of the actor playing the scout was a small wooden board that the arrow must hit. The target was not only small, it was moveable.

Robin Hood sees the scout coming out from behind a tree, and the shooting begins.

So far, we have had detective problems and problems in cinematography. Now we will offer you a problem from the theater.

Problem 60
The flag of Gascon

Once there was a rehearsal of *Cyrano de Bergerac*, by Rostand. Beautiful decorations were made, and the actors played their parts very well — yet the producer was not satisfied.

"Here Gascon defies the enemy," he said to his assistant. "The flag is set on a tall flagpole over Gascon`s position. This is the center of the battle. But we cannot *feel* it."

"Why is that?" asked the assistant. "Cyrano is fighting under the flag."

"The flag is hanging motionless," said the producer. "It looks like a piece of cloth. The flag should fly in the wind!"

"How can we do that?" the assistant said spreading out his hands. "The stage is big, and we would have to install a huge fan in order to flutter the flag. The noise would be like an airport. I cannot think how to make that flag fly without a fan."

And here the inventor appeared.

"Of course the flag should proudly fly as if in a wind," he said. "There is a Patent #800332."

Problem 61
I am going to the toy store....

A big apparatus was developed and assembled in one of the Colleges of Physics. Its main part was a huge magnet 50 meters tall. The apparatus required great accuracy, so the magnet was perfectly straight and highly polished.

And suddenly the worst thing happened. A couple of kilograms of iron powder were found on the polished surface of the magnet. Physicists were very concerned. How could they clean that powder off the magnet? The magnetic field was holding every particle of iron so tight it was impossible to blow or wash the powder off. If a scraper was used, the polished magnet surface would be destroyed. Dissolving the powder with acid was no good because the acid would corrode the magnet.

And the inventor appeared, of course.

"I am going to the toy store," he said. "I will clean the magnet in half an hour."

This is a needless S-Field: Two Substances and the Field. In order to break up this S-Field we have to introduce a third substance. What kind of substance should be introduced?

The patent was issued on this solution to this problem. By the way, fourth grade students also solved this problem.

Problem 62
Lazurite for "Running on Waves"

In the story "Running-on-Waves," by Alexander Green, there was a beautiful memorial in Gel-Gue square of a mysterious woman running over the surface of the sea. One day a young sculptor appeared who wanted to erect exactly the same memorial as in that story. It was easy to make a statue of the woman — light, rushing, mysterious. Under her feet the sculptor decided to place a flat plate of Lazurite, a natural bluish-white stone that is reminiscent of a foaming ocean.

Fifty large stone blocks were delivered to his shop. The most efficient method was employed to form a cube out of the stone blocks. A torch was used to level the surface of the stone. Sharp, or uneven, edges were melted by the flame. The work, however, went slowly. It was necessary to remove the torch and check each surface periodically. The work was often interrupted out of fear that the overheated Lazurite might crack.

The sculptor was nervous. Green's memorial celebration was near, but "Running" could not be erected in the town square. Once, the sculptor's sixth-grade daughter offered a simple method to allow speeding-up the leveling process by a factor of ten. The speed of the work increased without interruption. Do you have an idea what the sculptor's daughter offered?

Problem 63
An ideal solution

Welding by friction is one of the most simple methods of connecting two metals. One piece of metal is placed in a fixed position while the other is rotated against it. As long as there is a gap between the metal pieces nothing happens. As soon as the parts are pressed together high heat develops in the area of contact, and the metal starts to melt. If we apply high pressure the two parts will weld together.

In a factory, a pipe line has to be built out of cast iron pipes 10 meters long. These pipes should be connected by welding them with friction. In order to turn these pipes, a huge machine must be built. The pipeline should go through several shops in the factory. The chief engineer decided to get advice from his engineers.

"We cannot change the method of welding," he said. "Welding by friction must be used. The welding machine cannot fit in the shops the pipeline has to go through."

"We can stop production in the first shop, dismantle the equipment, install the pipeline, and put the equipment together again. Then go on to the next shop," said one engineer.

"That won't work," said another engineer. "The shop will lose a lot of time. We can build the pipeline out of short pipes only 50 centimeters long. A smaller machine can turn the pipe. We could install the pipeline without disturbing the shop."

"That is no good either," replied the chief engineer. "With pipes of this length we will have a lot of seams, and the pipeline would be unreliable. Besides, we cannot change the project. It was decided the pipes should be 10 meters long, and that's how long they should be."

And suddenly the inventor appeared.

"I can offer an ideal solution," he said. "There is a contradiction here. The pipe *should* be rotated in order to be welded — and the pipe *should not* be rotated in order to avoid using a big machine. The ideal solution is: The pipe is rotated and it is not rotated. For that we have to...." What do you think?

Problem 64
A device that never fails

In a chemical processing plant a container is filled with a very corrosive liquid. The foreman complained to his boss: "I have to know how much liquid flows from the container into the reactor. We have tried different devices of metal and glass, but the liquid soon corrodes them."

"We now have metal containers that resist corrosion," the boss repeated. "We can order a device made of this metal."

"It will take too much time," said the foreman.

"What if we just measure the level of the liquid in the container?" asked the boss.

"We will not get the required accuracy," answered the foreman. "The level of the liquid changes very little. Just try to see it. Besides, it is inconvenient because the container is installed next to the ceiling."

And here the inventor appeared.

"My device will work forever," he said. "Try to measure not liquid, but...." Try to solve this problem.

Chapter 32
Keys to Problems

Now, let's work out problems stated in previous chapters. This will make it easier for you to solve other problems.

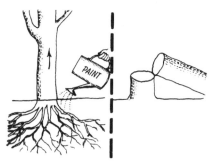

We will start with **Problem #11, painting children's wooden furniture.** The solution is to paint the tree before cutting it down. A paint solution is poured over the roots of the tree. The solution mixes with the tree's sap and spreads throughout the tree.

Problem #13, grinding glass sheets, is not difficult to solve. Temporary thin sheets of glass are packed in a thick bundle and ground together.

Problem #16 is about the airplane that made an emergency land-

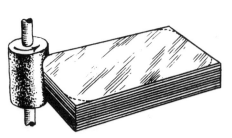

ing in a field. We should use a dirigible, and we should not use a dirigible. Two big elastic bags are placed under the wings and filled with air. These bags gently lift the airplane. Big platforms on wheels are placed under these bags. Now we can tow the airplane. *There is a dirigible, and there is no di-*

rigible — the airplane is supported by airbags.

Problem #20 is about the catamaran. It is also not complicated. If you remember, technical systems during the third stage of their development become more dynamic, more flexible, and more organized.

Inventor E. Lapin received Patent #524728 on the catamaran. It had two bodies connected with expandable poles allowing the bodies to be close to each other. This catamaran could also go through shallow parts of the river with greater ease.

Problem #24, about the dredging machine, has a similar solution. The pipeline should become more dynamic — more

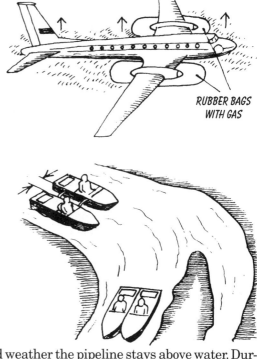

RUBBER BAGS
WITH GAS

flexible and moveable. During good weather the pipeline stays above water. During a storm, it goes underneath the water.

40 CM

12 CM

HELP

Problem #25 is about the propeller for Carlson. It also can be solved by transformation of the technical system into a dynamic and changeable one. The propeller should be big during flight and small on the ground. The blades of the prop can be made of thin, flexible strips which are then wound-up like a toy "tongue." While spinning, the blades of the prop will unwind and become full size blades. When the propeller stalls, the blades will curl back.

It is interesting that several inventors were issued patents on similar designs. To save drowning people, a long elastic pipe is curled into a roll. As soon as air is forced inside the pipe, it will unwind and stretch from the boat towards the drowning person.

Problem #23 is about a contour

line movie and is difficult. But you know the rule: Ferromagnetic powder introduced into a substance can act to control the substance's movements through a magnetic field. Instead of a cord, we can take a flexible tube and fill it up with ferromagnetic powder. We can even take a thread, soak it in glue, and cover it with powder. The thread is placed on a thin, insulated plate, and controlled by a strong magnetic field from underneath the plate.

Problem #26 is about the setting of diamond grains, and is more complex than the previous problem. Iron powder must be sprayed over the diamonds. With the control of a magnetic field, all diamonds will align top-up.

These problems are similar to **Problem #57** about the hunter and the dog. In order for a field to act on a substance, another substance should be added which can respond to that field. Another "substance" responding to the sound field should be added to the hunter.

Problem #27 is about packaging apples. Here we have to use the rule about breaking-up the S-Field. A third substance, also fruit-like, should be placed between two colliding fruits. Let's place two dozen ping-pong balls into a carton of apples. The balls will soften the impact of the apples. The carton is placed on a vibro-table. The balls, being lighter, will rise to the top of the fruit and take the abuse away from the falling apples.

The question arises: "What should we do with the balls after the carton is filled with apples?"

It is ridiculous to pick them out by hand and put them into another carton. The problem of how to move objects is already known to you. A steel plate is installed into the body of the balls. An electromagnet is placed above the carton. After the carton is filled, the electromagnet is turned on, and all the balls jump out of the carton. The conveyor removes the full carton and positions an empty one. The electromagnet is turned off and all the balls fall into the empty carton — and the cycle starts over again.

Problem #38 is about iron powder mixed with a polymer. This problem is similar to the one in the third chapter about oil. The answer is the same. An iron compound is used that breaks-up in hot polymer.

Problem #44, about the oil pipeline, is more complicated. There are liquids in the pipeline next to each other and they are separated only by a big rubber ball. Let us use Operator STC. In our mind, let us decrease the size of the ball. Instead of one big ball, we will use many tennis balls, or floating pellets. A patent on this type of plug was issued. This solution is very logical — a rigid system becomes more dynamic. This corresponds with the natural tendency of the development of technical systems.

If we continue the experiment we will have to make a transition from pellets to even smaller particles — molecules. A new idea now emerges: Make a plug out of liquid or gas. A gas "plug" cannot separate the oil because oil can pass through gas. But a liquid "plug" is possible. For example, one of the products is kerosene, then a "water plug," and then the other product is gasoline.

This water separator has a lot of advantages. It never sticks inside the pipeline or the pumping station. There is a disadvantage to using a water separator. The petroleum product before and after the "plug" will impregnate the inside of the "plug" and slowly mix with it. It will be difficult to separate the petroleum from the water at the final station, and this mixed "plug" must be thrown away.

Let us try to formulate the **IFR**. The liquid substance of the separator at the final station has to separate from the petroleum by itself. There are only two possibilities. Either the liquid becomes solid and settles down, or it becomes gaseous and evaporates.

Remember the old principle: Matter can be dissolved only within similar matter. Petroleum is an organic substance. We need a separator that will not dissolve in petroleum. Therefore the separator should be made of a non-organic liquid. It should be inexpensive, safe, and inert to petroleum. Having so many precise characteristics we can easily find the needed substance in a handbook. A **"separator"** made out of **Aqua Ammonia** will secure the separation of petroleum products and go through the pipeline without a problem. During transportation, this separator will partially mix with the petroleum. This is no real danger. At the final station, the ammonia will turn into a gas and evaporate, and the petroleum will stay in the reservoir.

After solving the "plug" problem, we can now attack **Problem #48 — the body of the ship**. Under the conditions of this problem the body of the ship should be flexible and moveable. Well, let us imagine that the body of the ship is made of liquid. This seems a crazy idea. But, we already have some expertise in the transformation of solid matter into liquid. At the same time, the model made of miniature dwarves can lead to this idea.

So, instead of a steel sheet, we will use a "liquid" one. The first concern is to protect the liquid from spilling. A flexible lining has to be installed — maybe one made of strong rubber — and must connected with partitions. This way the wall will look like hot water heating pads. It is funny, but some inventors think that the skin of dolphins looks like this.

Models built with this design create less friction during towing because they have less turbulence. However, these flexible skins are not as efficient as that of dolphins. Dolphins can change the shape of their skin by adjusting to different environments. The man-made skin is "dead," lacking movement. Another problem now appears: How can we control every part of this flexible skin?

Notice that, very often, one problem creates another. We must constantly move forward.

The problem about creating flexible skin can be easily solved because it is a problem concerning "relocation." You need to control the movement of the liquid under the skin. Let us build an S-Field: Ferromagnetic particles added to the liquid allow control with electromagnets. This patent, #457529, was issued not to ship builders, but to scientists.

One question remains: Can ships exist without a body? Such ships already exist, and you know about them — rafts. They have no body because wooden logs are the cargo, and during transit they become the body. British Patent #1403191 describes a ship with a long snakelike body made of steel boxes used as containers. The small "head" is the tugboat towing the long "body" of containers.

Chapter 33
Simple Rules

Perhaps the main, and most annoying, mistake of beginning inventors is their desire to achieve results while ignoring losses. Take for example **Problem #33 — the propane tank.** It is not difficult to measure the weight of the left-over liquid if, from time to time, you weigh the tank. But it is a very heavy tank, so this procedure is costly and inconvenient. A good solution is to have the tank signal when only a little gas is left.

Look at the drawing. The bottom of the tank is made with a slope, and a weight is installed in it. As long as the tank has enough liquid gas in it the tank will maintain a vertical position. When the gas reaches a lower level the weight will tilt the tank and thus signal the low level of gas.

Note that this result is achieved with practically no cost. There is no need to

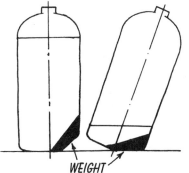

WEIGHT

change the gas tank. Install a wooden base with an asymmetrical weight — and the regular tank will become a "talking tank."

French inventors, who first thought about this, got Patent #456403 in the Soviet Union.

Problem 65
How can we help the workers

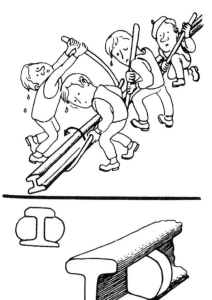

Perhaps you have seen workers move a heavy railroad rail. Several people set their crowbars underneath the rail and, at a command, flip it over and over until it reaches the right position. This is hard and dangerous work. If one worker dozes, the rail could pull the bar from his hand and.... How can we help the workers?

Let us use simple rules while working with this problem:

Rule #1: Before starting to solve the problem, determine why the problem occurs.

Indeed, why is it difficult to move these rails? Because they are heavy? However, a pipe of the same weight could roll over easily with little force applied. This means that the rail does not "know" how to roll.

Rule #2: State the contradiction.

The rail should be round in order to roll easily, and it should stay as a rail in order to be used as a railroad track. Here we have to use our imagination. We introduce contradictory requirements — the rail should stay a rail and at the same time should roll like a pipe.

Rule #3: Imagine the Ideal Solution (imagine yourself as a magician).

Turn on all your powers of imagination! The ideal solution will look like this: The rail, during relocation, becomes — as in a fairy tale — rollable.

If one eagerly tries to solve this problem without consideration of losses the answer is simple — place two wheels on the rail's ends. However, in order to do that, you have to lift the rail, and for that you need a lifting mechanism. Once again, only those solutions are good which allow you to reach a result without complicating the system, or without adding considerable cost.

Engineer B. Bogaenco received his Patent #742514 for a simple solution. Four magnetic half-rounded inserts, two on each side of the rail, temporarily make the rail round and help it roll. These inserts are easy to install and remove.

Now we are offering two more problems using these rules.

Problem 66
Microbe hunters

In a Research Laboratory, water is tested for microbes. A porous metallic plate is used to collect samples. The plate is dipped in water then pulled out. Blotting paper is then applied to one side of the plate. This paper soaks the water from the plate, and the microbes are left on the other side. The microbes can not get through the pores of the plate. This side of the plate is then placed under a microscope and the number of microbes counted.

Only ten analyses per day can be done this way in the lab. Then one day the program was changed and every day the lab would have to test 500 plates.

"Each test takes a lot of time," said the manager of the lab. "The plate should be divided into 100 strips and all strips should be checked out through the microscope. We have to find a way to do this without using the microscope!"

"Without the microscope?" asked another scientist. "We can do that only if each microbe was as big as a dime."

Everybody laughed.

And suddenly the inventor appeared.

"Let's use our rules," he said.

Rule #1: Find out why the problem occurred.

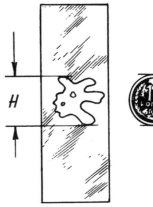
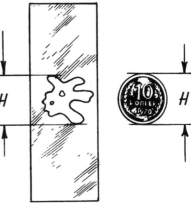

We have already determined this. Microbes are very small, and that is why we have to use a microscope — a very slow process.

Rule #2: State the contradiction.

Fine! Microbes have to be small — by nature invisible — and microbes have to be big in order to see them with human eyes.

Rule #3: Imagine the Ideal Solution.

Here it is: A microbe in water is small and, as soon as it comes out of the water, it increases in size.

"Thank you," said the manager. "Now we can solve the problem easily."

When working on this problem remember that optical devices — projectors, screens, and so on — cannot give you the necessary effect. A very simple device is required.

Problem 67
Grease with a secret

At a pipe-rolling mill, 10-meter pipes are produced out of red-hot steel plates. Fresh-made pipes, still very hot, need to be covered inside with a layer of grease several millimeters. How can we do that?

At first glance the problem seems a simple one. It is possible to use a platform on wheels that goes through the pipe and covers the surface with grease. Unfortunately, this solution is far from ideal. The speed of the production process will slow down and it will take a complicated machine to grease the inner surface of the pipe.

Several engineers recently received a patent on an invention which allows this process to be done fast and accurately.

Let's try to compete with this team! Think for a moment: Why did this problem appear?

There is nothing complicated about covering flat sheets with grease. But a pipe — a very hot pipe — is inconvenient for this type of work. Here is the contradiction: It is easy to grease a flat sheet; however, we have to grease a pipe — and a pipe is not flat! The sheet should be flat, and the sheet should be a pipe. The ideal solution is to grease *something* flat — not a pipe and not a steel sheet. That *something* should transfer grease into the pipe and . . . disappear.

These rules point in the general direction of the solution. The rest is up to your logic. Remember, it requires a solution close to the *ideal* one. The whole trick is that grease spreads over different surfaces. The pipe is still in the production stage, but the grease is already spread over another sheet — for instance over a paper roll! What is left is to transfer grease from this sheet onto the inside of the pipe. When this is done, the sheet "carrier" should disappear — burn — without any additional problems: Patent #804038. (Remember **Problems #5 and #15**).

Chapter 34
Cunning Plus a Little Physics

Here are some problems as exercises. Remember, you should try to find the answers not by guessing, but by using the rules and methods learned so far. If you have difficulties with the physics, consult a textbook for reference.

Problem 68
The Treasure of Pirate Flint

For a long time an expedition had been searching for Flint's treasure. Finally, with an underwater telecamera, the chest containing the treasure was found. This strong wooden chest was lying on the bottom of the ocean 500 meters deep. The chest was half buried in sand. After the initial excitement wore off, members of the expedition began to think about how to bring the chest to the surface. Usually, lost cargo was lifted with the help of pontoons. A pontoon is a closed metal container or tank. A pontoon filled with water is dropped into the

143

ocean and connected to the cargo. Then the water is displaced with compressed air and the pontoon rises lifting the cargo.

"*Piasters, piasters,*" said the head of the expedition gloomily. "But how can we lift those *piasters*? We have a pontoon, but how can we connect it to the chest? Divers can not go down that deep, and we do not have robots. All we have is an underwater telecamera and a pontoon."

And the Inventor appeared of course.

"Let us formulate the Ideal Final Result," he said. "The pontoon is lowered onto the top of the chest. This we can do without any problem because we have a telecamera. Our **Ideal Final Result** is: The top of the chest and the bottom of the pontoon, with nothing between them, must fasten to each other. Without anything — or with water, because there is a lot of water...."

How should we connect the pontoon and the chest with water?

Problem 69
Aibolit Needs a Thermometer

The conventional medical thermometer was invented a long time ago. It consists of a long plate with lines and numbers placed inside a glass test tube. A smaller glass tube with mercury is attached to the plate. When heat is applied, the mercury either expands and goes up or contracts and goes down inside the smaller tube. As you can see, the thermometer has a very simple design and this is its advantage. The problem is that it is difficult to read the position of the mercury inside the tube.

Do you remember what Doctor Aibolit did in Africa?

"Ten nights Aibolit
Didn't sleep, didn't drink, didn't eat,
He treated and treated sick animals
And gave them, and gave them
thermometers."

To look at thermometers ten nights in a row is not an easy task. It would be nice, if doctor Aibolit had a thermometer that had an easy-to-see column of mercury.

You have probably already thought about making the tube bigger in diameter. Unfortunately, in a wider tube, the column of mercury will go down by itself as soon as the temperature goes down. This is not acceptable for a medical thermometer.

So, try to think of a new thermometer. The characteristics of the old one should be preserved, but the column of mercury should still be seen easily.

Problem 70
Help the Sheriff

Here is a fragment from a detective story:

"We have caught you," the Sheriff said to the criminals. "And you are in the hands of the Law. You hoped to get away, didn't you? The *Jupiter* diamond is a good catch. We caught you with the evidence. Even though you have cut the diamond into several pieces, that will only increase your guilt."

"Do not be in a hurry Sheriff," said one of the convicts. "Did the *Jupiter* diamond disappear? We can only express our sympathy because we don't have this diamond. What we have are only five small diamonds — an inheritance from our grandma."

"That is exactly right," grinned another convict. "Look at this matter as a scientist. The weight is different, the shape is different, only the color is the same. There are a lot of white diamonds. The chemical composition is the same. Every diamond consist of carbon. It seems to me that you will have to let us go...."

Please help the Sheriff to unmask the convicts.

Problem 71
Coffee in weightlessness

In a space story, an astronaut decided to make coffee.

He asked himself how he could do it in weightlessness. "It is very simple," he thought. "I will take some liquid and magnetize it. Then I will take a metal cup with a long handle — and that's it! Now we are going to drink Turkish coffee from magnetic cups."

What do you think? Could he make coffee his way or not? What do you suggest? How can you make coffee in weightlessness? Keep in mind that it should be safe and simple — and of course the coffee should taste like coffee.

145

Problem 72
Building an S-Field

In a certain factory, workers digging in the ground found a pipeline.

"In what direction is the liquid flowing?" they asked.

They knocked on the pipe in many different ways and listened. They could not determine the direction of the flow.

"We will have to cut the pipe," said the engineer. "There is nothing we can do about it."

And the Inventor appeared, of course.

"Why should you cut the pipe?" he wondered. "What we have to do is finish constructing the S-Field. There are two substances: The pipe — S_1 — and the liquid — S_2. Now, the field should be added."

This is a simple problem, although a patent was issued on the solution.

Problem 73
Let's call the Firemen

The radio announced that Fall freezing temperature was coming.

"It is a disaster," said the director of the farm. "What can we do with our experimental area? We have plants that need a warm temperature."

"The area is big, and we can neither cover it with film nor heat it up," said the agriculturist.

And the Inventor appeared.

"Do you need to preserve heat in a big area?" he asked. "Call the firemen, I have an idea."

Why do you think he called for firemen?

Problem 74
It turns off by itself

An electric soldering gun was demonstrated at an exhibition. The gun would turn off automatically as soon as it was overheated.

"How does this gun work?" asked one of the visitors.

"There is probably a transducer that measures the temperature," suggested another visitor. "During overheating the transducer sends a signal and a special relay turns off the gun."

And suddenly the Inventor appeared.

"There is no transducer, nor relay." he said. "The gun turns off by itself. The trick is that...."

Problem 75
It is going to be inexpensive

In a tenth grade physics textbook, different electrical condensers are drawn. The simplest is made of two metal plates with an insulator — for instance, air. The smaller the gap, the greater the capacity of the condenser. School devices were made for demonstration purposes using a condenser with a moveable plate. The movement was achieved by a microscrew.

"That is very bad," said the director of the factory. "The plates are inexpensive, but the microscrew is very expensive."

"What can we do?" argued the chief engineer. "An experiment requires a very precise movement of the plate."

And the Inventor appeared.

"The condenser will be inexpensive. For that we have to take...."

What did the Inventor offer?

Problem 76
"I saw a funny picture..."

In a fur factory the treatment process of fur must be improved. During the process the fur skin is cleaned in a special liquid and rinsed in water. Then it is dried under a fan with warm air. The problem is that the stream of air dries the top of the fur where a hard crust of sticky hair develops. Underneath the crust there is still a lot of water. Engineers changed the temperature and velocity of the air, but nothing improved.

And the Inventor suddenly appeared.

"I saw a funny picture in a magazine," he said. "A barber gave his client a very scary story to read. The hair of the client stood on end and the barber did his job with ease."

"What are you going to offer to our furs?" asked the employee in wonder. "Do you suggest that our staff should read scary stories or show horror movies?"

"No, everything is really simple," answered the Inventor. "The hair will stand on end if you use a special physical effect."

147

What kind of effect was the inventor talking about?

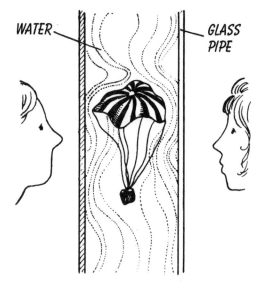

WATER

GLASS PIPE

Problem 77
The second half of the secret

Engineers studying different styles of parachutes made a small model of a parachute and placed it in a glass tube. A stream of water ran through the tube, and the engineers studied the behavior of the model and the development of turbulence in the water. The work did not go smoothly because of difficulty seeing colorless vortices in a colorless stream of water. Should we add some ink to the water? But, dark vortices in a dark stream will not make any difference.

Somebody offered to paint the model with a thin layer of soluble paint. The result was successful only for a while. In the colorless stream, the now colorful vortices stood out well. However, after ten minutes, the paint dissolved completely from the model and the test was temporarily stopped. When engineers painted the model with a thick layer of paint the shape of the model was distorted and the test lost its meaning.

"The paint should come from inside the model," said one engineer. "The parachute shroud wires are too thin. I cannot think how to make an inner channel small enough for the ink to pass through. We know of craftsmen that can make a picture on a grain of rice. Maybe we could find somebody like that."

"Can you imagine how much time it will take to make this model?" laughed another engineer.

And here the Inventor appeared.

"Let's try to fantasize a little bit," he said. "Here is a piece of wire for our model. It has no paint, and the shape of the model is not distorted. Let us dip the wire into the stream of water — and, on the surface of the wire, like in a fairy tale, there appears a thin layer of paint. The water washes this layer away and another layer comes out. This is an ideal solution. One thin layer replaces another."

"It is impossible," said the engineers. "Where will the paint come from?"

"From the water," answered the Inventor. "It has only one source. When water makes contact with the wire it turns into a paint, or a substance that differs from water in color. This is half of the secret. The second half is how to accomplish this."

148

Try to solve this problem yourself.

Last problem
Problem 78
Petals execute the command

A long time ago, from dawn to dusk, bees and other insects — pollinators — flew through the fields. Today, fertilizers are used in fields and they scare away insects.

Someone thought of a way to use strong wind instead of bees. Let the wind blow the pollen from flower to flower. One institute developed a huge fan that was brought to a field and turned on. Now there was wind, but no pollen — the petals closed from the wind and hid the pollen inside.

"It is understood that, during millions of years of evolution, plants developed a reaction causing them to close their petals while the wind blows," said a scientist. "Our wind is a signal to the flowers that bad weather is coming. Plants cannot understand that we are trying to help them."

"What can we do?" a colleague asked. "We cannot breed new plants. It will take years."

And here the Inventor appeared for the last time.

"Let us use a physical effect that you know very well," he said. "The petals will stay open all the time while the wind blows."

What do you think the Inventor had in mind?

149

Chapter 35
Learn to Invent

The history of mankind begins with invention: The first stone tools were developed and Homo Sapiens — thinking man— appeared on the Earth.

It is impossible to count how many inventions have been made since that time. Everything that surrounds us was invented. For instance, we do not know who invented the sail — the most significant invention of the human race. This invention survived thousands of years and always will be with us. There are projects with space ships having solar sails.

Can you imagine how that inventor felt setting up sail for the first time? Probably, it was a sunny, windy day. The first puff of wind filled the rough woven mat-sail, and the raft, shuddering for the first time, broke away from the land. The first mast in history started to bend and squeak. Sunlight danced on the waves, but the sailor paid no attention. His heart beat furiously. He did not know where the raft would land, and it was frightening to look back. But it did not matter — here was the wonderful, insane moment of victory! For the first time the wind worked for humanity, and the raft moved forward loudly crashing against the waves.

The development, testing, and implementation of inventions always involves adventures. Victory over a technical problem takes flexibility of the brain and bravery — no less then it took D'Artagnan to overcome the machinations of Cardinal Richelieu. By the way, a technical problem can sometimes be trickier, and more powerful, than all Cardinals.

If you are looking today for adventures that are useful for the human race, **invent!**

In Technical Creativity you will have a lot of fascinating adventures — enough for the rest of your life. You have to start preparing yourself for such activity from an early age. The earlier the better, just as in sports. So do not lose any time.

I wish you success!

A note that could not fit in the margins:

Invention, discovery

An invention has to possess four characteristics: It should be a technical solution of the problem, it should be new, it should be substantually distinct from already known solutions, and it should produce a useful effect.

For example, a new method to train animals is not an invention because there is no technical solution to the problem. A bicycle with four or five seats is not an invention either because these bikes were developed in the last century.

Let's combine a paint brush with a shovel. It appears to be something new. But both the brush and shovel are used the same way. This new combination does not produce any new quality. If there are no new, significant or distinct qualities, there is no invention.

You can see now that before an idea is accepted as an invention it has to pass four severe tests. Patent applications are checked by patent examiners. Every year, the USSR registers more than 100,000 inventions.

Very often an invention is confused with a discovery. An invention can only be something that does not exist yet. For example, the first airplane was an invention.

Discover means to find something that already existed in nature but was not yet known. Gravity is not *invented*, it is *discovered*. Newton's Law, Ohm's Law, the decomposition of water into hydrogen and oxygen, and so on, are discoveries.

From 1959. In the Soviet Union, discoveries have been registered. During this time, there have been about 300 discoveries.

Now, you can determine whether or not the following items are inventions or discoveries:
1. Lathe machine
2. Smelting iron from steel.
3. Body inertia.
4. The relationship between a pendulum's oscillation and its length.
5. A clock pendulum.

Chapter 36
Into the Inventor's Card Index

Make an index card! Jules Verne did not patent his ideas, he just simply described them in his novels. In order to develop his technical and scientific knowledge, Jules Verne — starting in his youth and lasting throughout his life — collected new technical and scientific information from books, magazines and papers. Biographers state that his card index contained more than 20,000 entries with information about technology, geography, physics and astronomy.

Today many inventors maintain their own index cards. These cards contain information about physical, chemical and geometrical effects. There are also descriptions of successful methods and inventive tricks — information about new materials. In other words, everything that can contribute to the solution of a technical problem.

Index cards slowly accumulate and become very helpful during the search for new ideas. Sometimes an old forgotten card immediately helps solve a complicated new problem.

There is a piece of paper among my index cards with an extract from a book that is 100 years old. The book is called *Magic of the World* and was published in 1886.

Here is an extract from that book:

#89. Instant blossoming of a flower under the influence of electricity.

The magician takes a fresh-cut bud of any flower (a rose with the cut end of the stem covered with wax is best) and shows it to the audience in order to prove there is nothing inside the bud. Then he removes the wax, inserts a thin, long wire inside the stem, and installs the stem in a hole on the table, all the while describing what he is doing so that everyone can see that the flower is unchanged.

After that he signals his assistant, who connects a battery to the wire, and the current travels through the stem into the bud. And, under the great power of electricity, the bud opens up very fast in front of the eyes of the amazed audience.

One hundred years ago it was almost a super-trick, but today, in physics classes we learn that identically charged particles repel. The magician charged the petals with an identical charge. That's the whole trick!

This simple trick, however, solves **Problems #76 & #78**. The hair of the fur will stand on end if an identical charge is applied (Patent #563437). And, petals with identical charges will stay open in spite of the wind (Patent #755247). They are modern inventions made with the help of old tricks.

The inventor listens to the "pulse."

How can we determine if there is a crack in a ball bearing while it is working? The "healthy" bearing has one frequency of oscillation — it may be measured before the test. A cracked bearing has a different frequency because the bearing now is actually divided in half.

In the past few years many patents were issued for similar inventions. The polishing process of metal belts had to be interrupted in order to measure their thickness. Now the thickness is measured continuously by measuring the vibration frequency of the belt while it is placed inside the acid solution for processing.

Doctors measure the pulse of the human body to determine its condition. Frequency of vibration is like a pulse — it tells about the health of parts of a machine, or of the machine in general. When the length, mass, pressure — and so on — change, so does the frequency.

It is a bad doctor who does not know anything about a patient's pulse.

Now, a simple task: A pole is driven into the ground. How can we determine how firmly the ground is holding it?

Balls, water and fantasy

In many countries people have thought about how to reduce the waste of oil from large open reservoirs. Indeed, in the summer, reservoirs are heated by sun light and a lot of oil evaporates. It seems easy to protect the oil with a floating "cover." This "float" would go down as the level of oil goes down. But the problem is that the walls of the reservoir are not straight. This creates gaps between the float and the walls, letting oil evaporate. People have designed covers with flexible sides which were complicated and expensive. Here is a technical contradiction: Reducing the waste of oil complicates the construction of the cover. A very simple solution suddenly appeared. Cover the surface of the oil in the reservoir with floating balls smaller than tennis balls. The balls will cover the oil very securely, and they take on the shape of the reservoir.

Isn't this a smart solution?

The ingenuity of the inventor appears when he solves a complicated problem with a simple solution.

Now, try to imagine a plant that has a process for covering metal parts with Chrome or Nickel. Instead of machines there are big tanks where the parts are dipped. There is a solution of harmful liquids inside. What should we do? Make covers? But those parts go in and out all the time. Covers would be interrupting the process. Here is a contradiction again. This is similar to the previous one, and it should be solved the same way. You have probably figured it out. The tank should be covered with a layer of balls. This cover will seal the tank and prevent the liquid from splashing.

Recently, one steel plant had to lay out thick metal sheets. During this process the sheets had to be moved and turned. How is that possible if the sheet weighs 1.5 tons and is 6 meters long? Once again, floating balls helped to solve this problem, because every ball can carry some weight. There could be many balls and their sizes might vary so they can carry a heavier loads. This is how the idea of the floating conveyor was originated. The simplicity of this conveyor surprises us. Water runs down through the trough and the hollow metal balls floating on top of the water receive the load. These balls carry the weight, that's all.

A bag + air.

How can we transport fragile glass devices by railroad cars? Twenty years ago, inventors suggested the use of plastic bags for that purpose. Air is pumped into the bags, and the product is secured very safely for transportation. "Bag + air" is a very simple and handy mechanism. It is not sur-  prising that inventors started using this mechanism to solve different problems where two objects are held against each other. For instance, it was necessary to hold a very brittle object tightly while it was sawed. The air bag is

154

used - Patent #409875. One plate of a powerful electric switch has to be pressed against another: The air bag is used - USA Patent #3305652. Even the heavy gypsum cast applied to broken bones has been replaced with "air bags."

Now the question is: Can we make improvements on "air bags"?

You know a very powerful method: Iron powder added to a substance and acted upon by a magnet or electromagnet.

Recently, a new invention appeared (Patent #534551). Iron powder was placed inside an air bag and an electromagnet was used from the outside to activate the powder. The air bag thus got new properties. It was now possible to adjust the pressure of the air bag to properly "press" an object. At first the new air bag was used only to hold parts during a grinding process. It is not difficult to imagine that inventors will also magnetize other types of air bags.

Invented by Nature

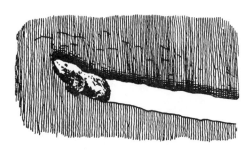

What should a machine that moves inside the earth look like? This question was published in the magazine *Pioneer Truth*.

Here is a typical answer: "Take a tractor and install shovels in front of it to cut the ground."

This mechanism has to shovel a lot of dirt just to move a couple of meters. A tractor is too big, and was not made to move in a narrow space. Machines made to do one type of work cannot be used in a different environment. Other people offered underground vehicles with wings. Why?

In all the projects on underground vehicles, the machine moves dirt from the front to its rear. The mole — a living underground machine — works differently. The mole leaves an empty tunnel behind him in order to easily get back. About 20 years ago, engineer A. Trebelev conducted an experiment with moles before he developed an underground vehicle. He found that the mole turns its head all the time pressing the dirt into the wall of the tunnel. Several years ago, Soviet engineers got their patent on a "man made mole." At the front of that machine they installed a cutting cone that not only breaks-up dirt but, like the mole's head, compresses the particles into the wall of the tunnel.

As you see, inventors should not only know technology, but should learn about nature as well.

Bypass Archimedes' principle

When Alex Zdun-Pushkin came to the Baku Institute of Technical Creativity, the Admitting Committee was confused. The question was whether or not an eighth-grade student could be enrolled in a class with engineers and other professionals.

Alex had been studying methods of technical creativity for two years. He had solved many problems, and learned about patent funds. Soon he sent in a patent application for a new solution to a technical problem and was awarded a patent.

This is his invention: Imagine a float in a tank with water. The float supports part of a machine. According to Archimedes' law, the supporting force is equal to the weight of the water displaced by the float. What if we need to increase the supporting force by 10 times? There is no room to make the float bigger. Can we replace the water with a heavier liquid? That is very expensive, and the supporting force will increase only by two or three times. The Archimedes principle should be bypassed. But, how?

The idea of Alex's invention is that if one adds a fine powder of iron to the water and starts to treat this water with a magnetic field, the specific gravity of the water will increase by 10 to 12 times.

Based on that invention, he got his diploma at the Institute of Technical Creativity.

The sun caresses the wings

There are inventions whose fate reminds one of Anderson's Tale about the ugly duckling. They are also kicked, laughed at, and pecked....

The first steamboat that crossed the Atlantic Ocean covered more than half the distance under sail. The boat had no passengers nor cargo. All the space was filled with coal, and in spite of that, there was not enough fuel to cover the whole distance. Major newspapers wrote: "Steamboats cruising across the ocean are nonsense. The ships can carry only their own fuel!"

The first vacuum cleaner was built in 1901, and it could barely fit into a horse carriage. This contraption would come to a house where workers would unwind its hose and stretch it out into a room As soon as they started the engine and began cleaning, a laughing crowd would immediately gather around throwing stones at the machine....

The first pocketwatch was so heavy that it was impossible to carry in your pocket. Owners very often would hire a butler to carry the watch. This provided a lot of laughs.

The energy of the first solar engine was barely enough to run a small printing press. On cloudy days the paper could not be printed. This was cause for many jokes, caricatures and laughs. Was the idea to use solar energy a mistake? In our time, solar elements work on many installations — including spaceships.

New machines should not be judged by their looks but by the power of their ideas. Days will pass, and the "ugly duckling" will become a "beautiful swan." And, as Andersen said, old swans will bow their heads before him and the sun will caress his wings.

A ship in tiger's skin

An inventor, G. Sutiagin, offered to cover the outer sides of a ship with tiger skins, thereby reducing friction between the ship, water, and air. Imagine a harbor with this type of vessel; ocean liners covered with leopard's furs, high-speed boats covered with synthetic tiger's skin, heavy tankers with bear's furs.

Yet it does make sense to consider this idea when making sports boat prototypes.

The ocean has to stay clean.

Thor Heyerdahl was surprised to see pollution throughout the Atlantic Ocean during his voyage on RA-1 and RA-2. Oil spills sometimes spread from horizon to horizon. About one percent of all oil transported spills into the sea — millions of tons. Inventors have put a lot of effort into solving these pollution problems. People try to burn the spills, or collect the oil with giant plastic sponges. One of the most interesting methods is to cover the oil spills with magnetic powder. This mixture, having magnetic properties, could be collected by large magnets.

Today, the size of oil tankers is increasing. Recently, a large, halve-million ton, tanker had an accident. Fortunately it was empty. What would have happened had it been full? How could we collect this giant oil lake? There is still no satisfactory solution. Inventors continue to search.

Fairy tales are not true, but they do contain hints

At first glance, the story told by Captain Vroongel (*Liar*) is absolutely unreal. But, if you search hard, you can find grains of inventive ideas, just as in the stories of Baron Munchausen. There are many inventive ideas in books about Gulliver, Alice in Wonderland and the Little Prince.

Writers make up very unusual stories. Sometimes they create hopeless situations for their heroes to somehow later find a way out. Comic books can not only make us laugh, they can also teach us to think about how to get out

of unpredictable situations.

Do you remember what happened to Captain Vroongel in Canada? He had to reach Alaska by sled. A group called "Misfortune" bought a deer and dog only to suddenly realize that the "deer" was really a cow, and the dog was really a wolf. Vroongel found a very smart solution. He harnessed the dog behind the cow, and the frightened cow drew the sled at greater speed.

A similar story happened to Baron Munchausen when he was chased by a lion, and found a crocodile in front of him. Munchausen invented a way to combine two minuses so that they destroyed each other.

In inventive theory, this method is stated as follows:

> **Harmful factors can be combined in such a way as to cancel each other out.**

We can give an example to support this rule:

Doctors trying to find a way to remove a red birthmark on the skin, tried several different methods. Nothing worked. Then they used the Vroongel and Munchausen rule to solve the problem. They injected green color under the skin. The green color by itself would stay green, but, in reaction with the red pigment of the birthmark, green and red neutralized each other.

One does the work of two

"MISFORTUNE"

A good inventor has his own inventive signature. There is a signature that belongs to Vroongel. Most of Vroongel's tricks were created when he let an object play a

158

double role: A life saver becomes a collar, the copper letters "Misfortune" become horseshoes, a fire extinguisher becomes a gun to fight a snake, and even squirrels replace an engine....

To force one object to do double work is a very strong, and widely used, inventive method. When the Soviets developed the space station "Venice-12," at the last moment they needed to add one more device weighing 6 kg. The designers did not want to hear about it, because every kilogram was already calculated into the weight of the ship. However, a solution was found — an exact recipe once used by Captain Vroongel.

Sand, or water, is loaded into the hold of ships returning without cargo. This is to make the vessels more stable. Vroongel once took on dirt as ballast. At the same time, the ballast was also soil for the palm tree used as the ship's mast.

Thus, on one part of the spaceship "Venice-12," a ballast was needed in order to control the ship's landing direction. Instead of ballast, the above mentioned additional 6kg device was installed. It worked both as a device and as ballast.

"Place the head on the fence."

Do you remember when Alice met the strange Knight in the world through the looking glass?

"I invented a new method for going over a fence," the Knight said. "Would you like me to tell it to you?"

"Please," said Alice politely.

"Here's how I came-up with the idea," the Knight continued. "I thought that the main difficulty is in lifting-up one's legs. After all, one's head is already over the top. If we stand on the fence with our head, our legs will now be on top, correct? And the next thing you know, you're over the fence...."

Alice could not believe the Knight — he was full of crazy ideas. Yet, this strange way of going over a fence is also a very interesting invention. Soviet inventors G. Katis and I. Melnichenko built an all-terrain vehicle that used this same principle. This vehicle consisted of two carts connected with a frame. One cart rests over the other. When the vehicle reaches an obstacle it places its upper cart on it. As the Knight mentioned, this is not difficult to do. Now, the cargo is moved through the frame from the lower cart to upper cart. The lower cart is then lifted on to the top of the frame, and the vehicle travels forward.

Does an inventor need science fiction?

One day a letter came to the publisher of the magazine *Pioneer Truth* saying that there was a debate in the classroom as to whether or not students should read science fiction stories. Many students said it was a waste of time because such stories were not real. This opinion is very common — and is a mistake. Science fiction writers are trying to see the future, even when it is so remote it is not realistic. They have described airplanes, submarines, television, and more when nothing like them had as yet existed on earth. Writers have written stories about journeys into solar systems, about robots, about the reconstruction of the human body. Today, many of these ideas have become reality. Science fiction is a searchlight into the future. Those who go to school today will live in that future. There is unreal fantasy, too, of course. But even that is very useful because it helps to develop imagination and teaches us to think freely. It is impossible to go to the moon inside a gun shell. However, Konstantin Tsiolkovsky wrote that the first ideas about rockets came to him after reading a novel by Jules Verne called "From Cannon to the Moon." Fantasy is needed in order to make real inventions and discoveries.

The power of mind

Fantasy is mobility of thought. The contemporary inventor has to read books about science fiction because they reduce psychological inertia and increase the power of imagination. Fantasy can be developed using the methods described in this book: Operator STC, MMD and IFR.

We live in an "Era of Technical Revolution." The main point is that this revolution lies not in the appearance of new machines — that has happened before. The method of developing new machines is changing. Organized ways of thinking replace the old chaotic ones. Every step in the thinking process should be as accurate as the movements of a pilot flying an airplane.

At the dawn of the human race, mankind conquered fire. Now we are learning to conquer something much greater: The power of mind capable of penetrating an unknown future.

Appendices

Appendix 1
Answers to Problems

1. To break or not to break? Apply a Corona Discharge effect to measure the pressure of the gas inside the light bulb.

2. There is a "trick" involved ... Freeze the liquor syrup and dip the syrup icicle into melted chocolate

3. What place should we choose? Use a waterleveling device.

4. "A" and "B" were sitting on a fence. Apply a different charge to droplets A(+) and B(-) so they can be attracted mutually.

5. It can disappear by itself. Use dry ice. After it cleans the parts, then it will evaporate.

6. There is a patent. Freeze the rubber, then drill the holes.

7. What kind of detectives are they? Suspend a bucket inside the tank before filling the tank with oil.

8. Vehicle for planet Mars. Fill the tires with stones or steel balls.

9. One as good as many. Divide the flow into 2 streams and charge one stream positive, the other - negative.

10. To make water softer. Add air into the water - gassify water.

11. Everlasting paint. Water the plant with dye additives that will bring

Missing answers to Appendix 1

12. Droplets on the screen. Turn the light on and off with the frequency of 24 times per second.

13. Thick and thin. Temporarily glue a number of glass sheets together and grind them as a stack.

14. How to get out of dead end. Heat sheets of metal in the induction chamber. Inner layer will be hotter than the surface.

15. Stubborn spring. Freeze the spring in dry ice, place it in the device, and let the ice evaporate.

16. After an emergency landing. Install rubber bags underneath the wings and fill them up with light gas.

17. A thermometer for weevils. Place many weevils inside the glass and use a regular thermometer.

18. The other way around. Make a glass filter out of thin glass rods.

19. Let's do it without telepathy. Drop a small buoy inside the gas tank.

20. There is a catamaran; there is no catamaran. Two floats of a catamaran are connected with expandable rods.

21. The law is the law. It is possible to create different variants. One is to have two pendulums that could generate complex oscillations that are not predictable.

the color inside the plant cells.

22. The universal field. Mix metal powder with the soil and control it with a magnetic field.

23. Wait, Rabbit, I will get you! Use a ferromagnetic powder and control it with a magnetic field.

24. In spite of all storms. Lower the pipelines underneath the water surface.

25. Propeller for Carlson. Make the propeller out of thin, flexible wound up strips.

26. Ten thousands pyramids. Use a ferromagnetic powder and a magnetic field

27. An almost excellent machine. Place light balls with internal metal plate into the carton.

28. There is no fountain like that. Unification of the system. Union with emptiness. Fountains with a mist or bubbles. We must be able to control the bubble development.

29. It is going to work forever! Install a magnet on the outside of the elbow, develop a protective layer out of steel balls.

30. Super precision valve. Use the heat expansion effect for precision flow control.

31. Let's look into the future. 1. Piezoeffect; 2. Magnetostriction; etc.

32. Ice on the electric power lines. Place magnetic rings over the wire that will develop an electromagnetic induction.

33. The tank reported politely. Place a propane tank in the cradle with an offset balance.

34. Where the wind blows from. Use soap bubbles.

35. Invention by request. Use the Corona discharge effect to control the diameter and the shape of the wire.

36. An accuracy within one degree. Mix the grain with magnetic powder that has the needed Curie point of 65 F.

37. Let's throw the screw out. Heat Expansion, Magnetostriction.

38. Something simpler. Mix iron powder with the polymer.

39. Powder on the conveyor. Use heavy oil or foam.

40. Stop guessing. Use water over the hot clinker to develop a foam cover.

41. Let us discuss the situation. A tray with melted tin is used to support the hot glass ribbon.

42. Rain is not a hindrance. Two air sacks are used to cover the opening of the compartment

43. Investigation is done by ex-

perts. Use the magnetic memory of steel.

44. A fresh idea is needed. A petroleum liquid separator can be made out of aqua ammonia. At the reservoir of the last station ammonia will evaporate by itself.

45. A capricious seesaw. Make the batcher more dynamic, design a moveable counterbalance in the form of a steel ball.

46. Contrary to physics. Use two substances, one that is heavier than the other.

47. Like in a fairy tale. Use a bimetallic spring to control the degree of the opening of the roof window.

48. Ships of the XXI Century. Make a flexible skin like a water bed filled with a magnetic liquid and control it with a magnetic field.

49. The train will leave in five minutes. Take a photo of the logs from the back of the car and measure the diameter of the timber according to scale.

50. A pound of gold. Build the testing sample as hollow cubes and pour the acid inside the sample.

51. The secret of the sleuth dog. Use a magnet inside of one of the sticks.

52. Dangerous planet. There is no definite answer except to study how the existing environment protects itself.

53. Icicles in a roof gutter. To build up S-Field we need a "Tool": string inside the spout.

54. The drop of paint is the main hero. Magnetic liquid added to complete F-Field (ferromagnetic field).

55. We can manage the drops. Add magnetic liquid and apply a magnetic field.

57. The hunter and the dog. Hunter needs the second dog that will pull him towards the sound of the barking dog.

58. No answer.

59. The arrow of Robin Hood. We have to complete S-Field. The arrow is made hollow inside for a nylon string, one end of which is attached to the wooden target on the stuntman, the other end - to the bow string.

60. The flag of Gascon Guardsmen. The flag mast is hollow with holes on the side for a small fan to blow air through the mast at the flag.

61. I am going to the toy store. Use modeling clay.

63. An ideal solution. In order to weld two long pipes we have to take a short piece of pipe and insert it between two long ones. Rotate the short pipe while pressing all pipes together until they weld.

64. A device that never fails. Measure the resonance frequency of the air above the acid level in the tank.

65. How to help the workers. Install magnet inserts.

66. Microbe hunters. The liquid should be heated to create bubbles that will work as magnifying glasses, then take a picture and count the microbes.

67. Grease with a secret. Use a paper roll covered with grease.

68. The treasure of pirate Flint. Freeze the contacting surfaces between the pontoon and the wooden chest.

69. No answer.

70. Help the Sheriff. Use an iron knife. If you place an iron knife on the diamond crystal, the knife will sink into the crystal, because iron will absorb carbon molecules.

71. No answer.

72. Finish constructing the S-Field. Heat the pipe and see the direction of heat transfer.

73. Let's call the firemen. The foam is an ideal blanket.

74. It turns off by itself. Use ferromagnetic material with the Curie point as a temperature control switch.

75. No answer.

76. "I saw a funny picture . . ." Apply an electrostatic charge to the fur in order to separate hairs for drying purposes.

77. The second half of the secret. Apply an electrolysis process. One of the electrodes is the parachute model. Bubbles will come out of the model showing the flow of water.

78. Petals execute the command. The petals should have a similar charge, like that which creates the repulsive force.

Appendix 2
Methods, Effects and Tricks

1. Do it inversely.
2. Change the state of the physical property.
3. Do it in advance.
4. Do a little less.
5. Matreshka.
6. Conflicting requirements are separated in time or in space.
7. All special terms must be replaced with simple words.
8. Incorporation of similar or different objects into one system.
9. Fragmentation, Consolidation.
10. Dynamization.
11. Add magnetic powder to the substance and apply a magnetic field.
12. S-Field modeling.
13. Self-service.
14. Heat expansion.
15. Transition from macrostructure to microstructure.
16. Effect of the Corona discharge.
17. Curie point of ferromagnetic materials.
18. Combination of various effects.
19. Geometrical effect of the Moebius Ribbon.
20. Geometrical effect of the Rotating Hyperboloid.
21. Ideal Final Result (IFR).
22. Introduction of a second substance.
23. Utilization of soap bubbles and foam.
24. Operator STC (Size, Time, Cost).
25. Model with Miniature Dwarfs (MMD).
26. Make a copy and work with it.
27. Build a model of the problem.

Appendix 3
Providers of TRIZ-based
Services in the USA

American Supplier Institute
17333 Federal Drive, Suite 220,
Allen Park, MI 48101
Tel. (313) 336-8877

Center for Technology
Commercialization, Inc.
NASA Regional Technology
Transfer Center
1400 Computer Drive,
Westboro, MA 01581-5043
Dr. William Gasko,
Co-Executive Director
Tel. (508) 870-0042

Goal/QPC
13 Branch Street,
Methuen, MA   01844
Bob King, Executive Director.
Tel. (508) 685-3900

Ideation International, Inc.
23713 Riverside Drive,
Southfield, MI 48034
Tel. (810) 353-1313.

Invention Machine Corp.
4 Cambridge Center,
Cambridge, MA 02142
Val Tsourikov, CEO and
TRIZ Expert.
Tel. (617) 492-1303.

Renaissance Leadership
Institute, Inc.
P.O. Box 659
9907 Camper Lane,
Oregon House, CA 95962
Jim Kowalick, President.
Tel. (916) 692-1944.

Strategic Innovation, Inc.
7591 Brighton Road,
Brighton, MI 48116
Steven Ungvari, President.
Tel. (810) 220-3807

Technical Innovation
Center, Inc.
714A Southbridge Street,
Auburn, MA 01501
Lev Shulyak, President and
TRIZ Expert.
Tel. (508) 832-0314.

TRIZ Consulting, Inc.
2310 NE 48th Street, Suite 734,
Seattle, WA 98105
Zinovy Roysen, President and
TRIZ Expert.
Tel. (206) 526-5646.

The TRIZ Group
30120 Northgate Lane,
Southfield, MI 48076
Victor Fey, President and
TRIZ Expert.
Tel. (810) 433-3075.

About the Author

Genrich Altshuller, the father of TRIZ (*Theory of Inventive Problem Solving*), was born October, 1926 in Tashkent in the former USSR. He spent many years in Baku and, since 1990, has resided in Petrozavodsk.

At the age of 14, Altshuller received his first "inventor's certificate" for designing an underwater breathing device that used hydrogen peroxide decomposition for generating oxygen. He constructed and tested the invention himself.

Altshuller served in the navy where, because of his invention skills, he became a patent inspector. It was there in 1946, while studying thousands of patents, that he identified the underlying patterns of invention and laid the foundation for TRIZ. Testing his theory, Altshuller made many military inventions, including a design for a mine rescue suit that won first place at the All-Union Competition.

After the war, Soviet inventive capabilities fell into decay. In response to this situation, Altschuller wrote to Stalin in 1948 criticizing the Soviet state's ability to develop inventive work. He offered solutions utilizing TRIZ concepts. In return, Altshuller was arrested and, after a year of interrogation and torture, was sentenced to 25-years imprisonment in Siberia.

While enduring the terrible conditions in the concentration camp, Altschuller continued to develop TRIZ. The camp included many scholars, scientists, artists and intellectuals. It was there that he worked out the details of many aspects of his new science of creativity. The frozen concentration camp became the first institute of TRIZ.

In 1954, after Stalin's death, Altshuller was released. Two years later his first publication on TRIZ appeared.

TRIZ schools began to appear throughout the USSR until 1974 when Altschuller and his disciples once again fell from grace with the Soviet Central Committee. Nevertheless, TRIZ flourished underground. Altshuller, excluded from teaching or publishing anything TRIZ related, supported himself by writing science fiction, or "adventures in ideas" and often thinly disguised TRIZ teachings, under the pen name "Henry Altov.." It was not until *perestroyka* that TRIZ was allowed to resurface, and its has since flourished.

In 1989 the Russian TRIZ Association was established with Altschuller as President.

About the Translator

Lev A. Shulyak, an inventor for almost four decades, was born in Moscow, USSR.

In 1954, he received his degree as a Mechanical Engineer from the Moscow College of Highway Construction.

He worked as a mechanical engineer on the construction of BRATSK, the biggest hydropower station of its time, helping to design, manufacture and implement the first automatic system for producing wet concrete mix.

In 1961 he bought Henry Altshuller's first book on the subject of inventing: *How to Become an Inventor*. This book helped him in the problem solving process and, within a year, he received his first patent for an electromechanical transducer.

Mr. Shulyak was invited to lead a group of mechanical engineers at the Moscow Orgenergostroy Project Institute. His group joined another team of engineers to develop concrete manufacturing plants with varying capacities utilizing current technology.

From 1961 to 1974, he received 15 patents on automatic control systems and mechanical equipment. These inventions helped save millions of rubbles in the construction of several hydropower stations.

In 1973, he completed his Masters Degree in Mechanical Engineering. The following year, he emigrated to the United States. Settling in Worcester, Massachusetts, Shulyak was employed by Norton Company as a Project Manager from 1976 to 1983. Using his knowledge in TRIZ he saved hundreds of thousands of dollars for this company by redesigning process equipment.

He has received four American patents on different consumer products, some of which he has successfully manufactured and marketed.

In 1984, Shulyak was the first person in the United States to teach engineers and children the TRIZ methodology.

In 1991, he founded the Technical Innovation Center and began teaching many courses on TRIZ-based Systematic Innovation (SI) to inventors, engineers and children. He also translated from Russian this book *And Suddenly the Inventor Appeared* written by Altshuller under the pen name Altov. The translation was first published in 1993.

Today Mr. Shulyak is dedicating himself to fulfilling his dream of building a Center for Innovation and Creativity. The Center will promote creativity and Systematic Innovation to children and industry alike.

171